Professional **Development** for *Successful* Classrooms

Improving Student Writing Skills

Garth Sundem, M.M.

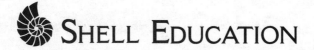

SHELL EDUCATION

Improving Student Writing Skills

Editor
Maria Elvira Kessler, M.A.

Project Manager
Maria Elvira Kessler, M.A.

Editor-in-Chief
Sharon Coan, M.S.Ed.

Creative Director
Lee Aucoin

Cover Design
Lee Aucoin
Lesley Palmer

Imaging
Phil Garcia

Lead Print Designer
Don Tran

Publisher
Corinne Burton, M.A.Ed.

Shell Education

5301 Oceanus Drive

Huntington Beach, CA 92649-1030

www.shelleducation.com

ISBN-978-1-4258-0377-3

©2006 Shell Educational Publishing, Inc.

Reprinted 2010

Table of Contents

Introduction 5

Vocabulary Review 7

Chapter 1: Your Physical Classroom 11
How Is Your Classroom Organized for Learning? 13
Basic Seating Arrangement 15
Seating Charts 16
Small Group Instruction Area 16
Daily Information Board 17
Storage for Writing Materials 18
Resource Materials 18
Supplies Checklist 19
Classroom Layout 20
Chapter 1 Reflection 21

Chapter 2: Frameworks for Classroom Time 23
Direct Instruction 24
The Writing Workshop 25
Adding Components to the Writing Workshop 28
   Author's Chair 29
   Journal Writing 31
   Assignment Packets 31
   Peer Revision 32
   Authentic Spelling 33
   Authentic Writing 34
Direct Instruction and the Workshop 37
Chapter 2 Reflection 40

Chapter 3: The Writing Process 41
Prewriting 43
Drafting 53
Revising 55
Proofreading/Editing 61
Publishing 62
Scaffolding the Writing Process 64
Chapter 3 Reflection 66

Table of Contents *(cont.)*

Chapter 4: Assessment and the Traits of Good Writing 67
Trait-Based Assessment 68
Other Assessment Strategies 69
    Holistic Assessment 69
    Portfolio Assessment 70
    Assignment-Specific Rubrics 71
The Traits Defined 72
Scoring the Traits 73
Common Difficulties with Trait-Based Assessment 90
Chapter 4 Reflection 98

Chapter 5: Teaching Using the Traits of Good Writing 99
Introductory Trait Lessons 100
Revision Directions for Introductory
    Trait Lessons 109
The Traits of Good Writing in Instruction 113
Monitoring Progress Through the Traits of
    Good Writing 116
Chapter 5 Reflection 121

Chapter 6: Assignments 123
Expository Prompts 124
Persuasive Prompts 125
Descriptive Prompts 126
Narrative Prompts 127
Daily Journal Prompts 128

Glossary 130

References 133

Introduction

As a writing teacher, you will need to make many choices. What will your classroom look like? What will you teach? How will you assess students' writing? There are many options, ranging from a book-centered approach that depends solely on direct instruction, to a writing workshop, in which students sit on couches and freewrite to the exclusion of instruction. Your preferences (and those of your district) likely fall somewhere between these two extremes and might use elements of each.

Also, teachers are becoming increasingly aware of the need to differentiate their instruction to meet the needs of diverse learners. Differentiation can be difficult—you will need to find ways to teach different skills in different ways to students with varying learning styles and abilities.

Finally, once you have a stack of finished assignments, what will you do with them? Experienced educators know that these assignments provide a useful window into students' skills, and that by assessing these assignments with a system that pinpoints the areas of strength and weakness, we can help students practice the areas where they need work.

It can be a little overwhelming at first. That is why this book gathers, as concisely as possible, today's proven best-practices in one place.

Within this book you will find:

- Practical strategies for immediately implementing best-practices writing instruction.

- A vocabulary review and glossary of relevant terminology covered throughout the book.

- Chapter reflection questions to help you pinpoint your own strengths and areas for improvement and to help you define your ideal classroom.

- Multiple approaches to writing instruction, allowing you to choose the strategies that work best for you and for your student population.

- In-depth descriptions of the Writing Workshop, Writing Process, and the Traits of Good Writing.

This book offers not only a compendium of useful strategies, but also the ability to assess your current classroom and teaching methods, using simple checklists, quizzes, and reflective questions. Presented in streamlined and ready-to-use format, the outlined techniques represent the cutting edge of today's best practices for writing instruction, stripped down to the components that will be physically used in the classroom. For a more in-depth look at these techniques and ready-to-use lessons to complement them, reference *Implementing an Effective Writing Program* (Pikiewicz & Sundem, 2004).

Vocabulary Review

As in any profession, writing instruction has its own vocabulary. Of course, knowing the terms is only one facet of being able to use the techniques you name; however, by naming and knowing the best practices, you take the first large step in using them to teach. Before reading any further, take a few minutes to write your definitions of the following terms in the spaces provided. After reading this book, revisit these terms and rewrite your definitions, adding any specifics you have learned.

Term	My First Definition	My Final Definition
assessment		
assignment packet		
Authentic Spelling		
Authentic Writing		
Author's Chair		
balanced literacy		
best practices		
bias in grading		
conventions		
descriptive writing		
differentiation		

Term	My First Definition	My Final Definition
direct instruction		
discovery-based learning		
draft		
editing		
expository writing		
flexible grouping		
grading		
holistic assessment		
ideas		
mini lesson		
narrative writing		
organization		
peer revision		
persuasive writing		

Term	My First Definition	My Final Definition
presentation		
prewrite		
progress		
publish		
revision		
rubric		
scaffolding		
sentence fluency		
Traits of Good Writing		
voice		
word choice		
writing process		
writing workshop		

Your Physical Classroom

Your classroom environment can define not only how your classroom will "feel," but can also help you implement different types of writing instruction. For example, you might choose to use the space around your walls as permanent learning centers, or you might instead leave this space empty, allowing for room to spread out students' desks. You might designate a section of your classroom to house reference materials or to use for small group instruction. You might even throw cushions in this space and use it as a reward reading nook. The choice will depend on what type of instruction you use in your classroom.

In addition to large-scale functionality, the materials you provide can contribute to or detract from the efficiency of your instruction. Will students who forget their pencils need to interrupt your lesson to ask if they can go to their cubby or locker, or will these students sign out a pencil from an organized materials area, knowing they will pay for it with clean-up time during a break? Likewise, will you provide students with the art materials they need to illustrate and publish their work, or is this a step that you will ask students to accomplish at home or in the school computer lab?

Researchers have noted that "good design does not happen accidentally, and when classroom designs are in the planning stages, the first priority should be the needs of the students" (Rogers, 2005, p. 1). Conscious design in general, and classroom design in particular, is the first step toward effective instruction.

How Is Your Classroom Organized for Learning?

Directions: Define your classroom organization priorities by circling the number that best represents how you feel about each choice (with "1" strongly agreeing with the opinion on the left and "10" strongly agreeing with the opinion on the right).

1	**2**	**3**	**4**	**5**	**6**	**7**	**8**	**9**	**10**

1 2 3 4 5 6 7 8 9 10
Students feel comfortable in my classroom.
The classroom promotes on-task behavior.

1 2 3 4 5 6 7 8 9 10
Students will learn to bring necessary writing supplies to class.
I will save instructional time by providing supplies if needed.

1 2 3 4 5 6 7 8 9 10
Students will need to move around during class.
Once seated, students should remain so.

1 2 3 4 5 6 7 8 9 10
I plan to have reference materials and research resources available.
Students will be responsible for the majority of research as homework.

1 2 3 4 5 6 7 8 9 10
My classroom needs to be partitioned to facilitate small group interaction.
Most of my assignments will be individual as opposed to collaborative.

1 2 3 4 5 6 7 8 9 10
Direct instruction will take the majority of class time.
Student exploration of assignments will take the majority of class time.

1 2 3 4 5 6 7 8 9 10
My classroom needs only to function for writing instruction.
My classroom needs to function for multiple subjects.

1 2 3 4 5 6 7 8 9 10
I prefer a quiet classroom.
I prefer a collaborative classroom.

1 2 3 4 5 6 7 8 9 10
I have extra space in my classroom.
Every inch of my classroom is used for seating.

1 2 3 4 5 6 7 8 9 10
I prefer an open, clean classroom with little distraction.
I prefer a classroom packed with creative influences.

How Is Your Classroom Organized for Learning? *(cont.)*

Directions: Reference the chart on the preceding page when answering the following questions. Take your time and answer each question honestly.

1. What trends do you notice in your preceding answers?

   _____

   _____

   _____

2. Which three choices are most important to you?

   _____

   _____

   _____

3. What three organizational tools will you use in your classroom to make sure each of these choices is as you wish?

   _____

   _____

   _____

4. Describe your ideal classroom.

   _____

   _____

   _____

Basic Seating Arrangement

The closer students are to one another, the more likely they will be to chat. Conversely, the more compartmentalized you keep students' space (i.e., in separate desks as opposed to tables), the less likely they will be to interact. Linda Shalaway observes that the days of 30 desks lined in neat rows facing the teacher's desk up front are long gone. She recommends clustered groups of four or a U-shaped configuration where everyone has a front row seat (Shalaway, 1999). There are many points in your writing class at which students will need to talk, for example, during peer editing, shared brainstorming, or small group instruction. Collaboration is a useful skill to foster, as well as a useful teaching technique, but left to its own devices it can encourage off-task behavior. Depending on your daily level of student-student interaction, you may choose to leave rows of desks as your standard and ask students to cluster their desks as needed, or you might use a "talking table" for group interaction in addition to student desks (this helps create a distinction between areas where students may talk and areas where they should be working independently). Leaving desks clustered as your norm encourages interaction, but can also be a distraction. Consider also including in your room a preferred seat or couch to which students can earn access by on-task behavior, exceptional writing, or simply on a rotation system (this is the positive motivation version of the outdated "dunce chair" at the front of the room—a disciplinary device that couldn't be more counterproductive).

In addition, many teachers utilize learning centers, which are areas of the room where students go to perform tasks such as collaborative editing, publishing (with organized supplies), brainstorming, small group instruction, etc. Managed efficiently, learning centers "provide children with opportunities for making choices, working with others, being involved in hands-on activities, and becoming fully engaged in learning" (Bottini & Grossman, 2005, p. 274). Like a designated talking table, learning centers can help ensure on-task behavior in the main seating arrangement by defining and separating the areas in which students may and may not interact.

Your other option, of course, is to populate your room with overstuffed chairs and couches (check your building regulations first!). For this, you will likely need to be an adept strategist or have a couple of years of teaching experience. However, a creative room can encourage creative writing—the final decision is, of course, up to you.

Seating Charts

The seating arrangement of your class can be one of the most powerful tools in encouraging consistent, independent work. Luckily, it is one of the easiest pieces to change as new personalities assert themselves, and you gain a clearer picture of your class dynamic. Generally, you will not want to cluster students who have difficulties focusing; however, isolating these students need not mean relegating them to corners or to the back of the class. Popular theory has held for some years that difficult students should, in fact, sit closer to the front. However, disruptive behavior up front will be seen by all and can be more disruptive than if the student is further back. Again, keep these ideas in mind and don't be afraid to let your seating chart evolve as your year progresses.

Small Group Instruction Area

Donald Graves (1989) notes that good classrooms have always stressed group as well as individual responsibility. One way to do this while also emphasizing differentiation is with an area of your room designated for small group instruction. This should be a creative area of your room where you can get together and make a bit of noise without disturbing other students who are working independently. If resources permit, use this area only for small group instruction and ask students to decorate the space, making it their own. Consider separating it from the main work environment with a stand-alone rack of books or small partition. As small group instruction will occur at every ability level, this should not be a stigmatized area of the room; rather, it can be a special place for intimate discussion (Radencich & McKay, 1995).

Daily Information Board

For each writing period, you will want whiteboard or bulletin board space to chart the day's activities. As students enter the classroom, they should reference the Daily Information Board instead of asking, "What are we doing today?" Figure 1.1 is an example of the type of Daily Information Board that might be used with a writing workshop.

Figure 1.1: Sample Daily Information Board

Introduction	Authentic Spelling: Test words/create new note cards	
Mini Lesson	Preview Author's Chair procedures	
Independent Writing	Class	Teacher
	Finish incorporating revision ideas, proofreading, publishing, and any outstanding activity sheets.	Help match writers with editors; distribute appropriate Peer/Adult Critique sheets.
Sharing or Wrap-up	Share a couple of Author's Chairs	

Storage for Writing Materials

Instead of asking students to complete work at home, many teachers now allow time for in-class completion (Hong, Milgram, & Rowell, 2004). This means that students will rarely have to transport their materials home, and you can organize students' writing folders in your classroom. Never letting student materials out of your sight helps to avoid lost assignments, misplaced drafts, and the dreaded homework-eating dog. Of course, if you choose to go this route, you will need a system for storing these writing folders. A good method is to use a storage box per class, in which you will file the folders alphabetically. Either decorate the boxes or encourage artistically talented students to decorate their class boxes; the second method gets you out of some preparation and helps students take ownership of their clasroom environment.

Resource Materials

In a designated area, organize dictionaries, thesauruses, stylebooks, English language usage guides, rhyming dictionaries, etc. For use in generating ideas, it is useful to have materials such as a book of world records, farmers' almanacs, and magazine collections such as *National Geographic*. The more books the better, as your goal is to immerse students in a literary environment (Morrow, 1997).

Supplies Checklist

Rather than wasting instructional time as students hunt for supplies, many teachers choose to keep an organized assortment of emergency writing materials. Consider asking students to "pay" for supplies with classroom cleanup time during a break or by helping with other organizational tasks. The list below represents supplies that you might consider keeping in your classroom. Create a list like the one below, and put a check next to the items/ideas you already have in your classroom. You could also put an "X" next to the ones you have decided against and an "O" next to the items you plan to include in your classroom but have not yet gotten. Once you get these materials, keep them organized where students can find them independent of prompting—the last thing you want is to spend your time retrieving supplies when you could be teaching. It is also a good idea to create a checkout list for students to sign when they borrow materials, in order to keep track of your materials.

✔	Supplies Needed
	Pencils
	Tape
	Writing pens
	Drawing pens
	White computer paper
	Construction paper
	Lined paper
	Scissors
	Dictionaries
	Thesauruses
	High-visual magazines
	Classroom fiction library
	Informative posters
	Ready-to-return box
	Computers
	Glue
	Red pencils
	Encyclopedias
	Almanacs

Classroom Layout

In the space below, draw the floor plan of your ideal classroom. How will you organize the primary learning space? Where will you store supplies? If you plan to partition your room, how will you do so and what will each space be used for? Where will your desk sit and will it be a focus? Where will you organize reference materials? If you are currently in a classroom, use this basic layout to start. If you like, create a checklist of ideas for use in designing your ideal space.

Chapter 1 Reflection

1. Describe how you plan to organize your classroom (seating, centers, supplies, etc.).

   _____

   _____

   _____

2. What do you see as the major instructional advantages and challenges of this system?

   _____

   _____

   _____

3. List elements of successful classrooms you have visited.

   _____

   _____

   _____

4. Ideally, what elements of classroom design will you work to include as the year progresses or in later years (i.e., what is your wish list)?

   _____

   _____

   _____

Frameworks for Classroom Time

The framework you choose for your classroom time will determine the majority of what you do on a day-to-day basis. Will students come to expect a period-long lesson with homework used to reinforce the learning? Will they expect to use the majority of the class period to work individually on their writing projects? Choosing a framework for your instruction will help you define your daily procedure and will help students become comfortable with the routine of your classroom.

Just as the writing process itself is cyclical (revisions might prompt additional brainstorming), so too does what you teach affect how you will structure your classroom environment. For example, in a classroom that depends exclusively on direct instruction (lecture format teaching), you may do away with a space for small group interaction. If you are teaching a writing workshop, you will need to set up your room for students to be comfortable during collaborative writing times, such as peer editing. Thus, after using this chapter to help you define your standard use of classroom instructional time, you may want to revisit the previous chapter.

On the following pages are three popular methods for organizing instructional time. Notice that while they are presented as distinct procedures, in actual practice you may draw from each. These techniques are not as black-and-white as they may seem at first. You will likely want to create your own guidelines for your use of classroom time, perhaps drawing from all three of those described below. However, taking the time to define your daily procedure can help you ensure efficiency and routine—both necessary to effective writing instruction.

Direct Instruction

While you want students to discover through experimentation which writing techniques work for their personal learning style, there is still certainly a need for direct instruction—you need not force students to reinvent the wheel of writing without first teaching them the skills that have proven successful over the years.

In its most basic form, direct instruction looks like the standard college lecture in which a teacher talks and students listen. During this time, students may take notes and discuss the learning with the teacher or as a class. At the end of direct instruction there is an easily defined skill or pool of knowledge for which the student will be accountable. In most direct instruction scenarios, you will want to assess student learning through a quick end-of-period discussion, quiz, or take-home assignment. As teachers, it is usually easy for us to rely on direct instruction, as it is the traditional technique by which we were likely taught while we were in school.

Also, direct instruction can be the easiest format in which to teach the maximum amount of information in the least amount of time (Kameenui, 1995), and it generally allows you to compartmentalize learning. For example, you could teach a period-long lesson on the elements of grammar, which students would understand independently of its application to writing (as seen on many standardized tests). As you can see, direct instruction relies heavily on creative lesson design and, if focusing on this technique, you will need to locate, organize, learn, and design interesting and engaging lessons for the majority of days spent in school.

When you think of a math class, you likely picture direct instruction. In fact, most writing textbooks still follow this model. For example, you may explain the use of parentheses and spend the remainder of the period completing an activity sheet that emphasizes the use of parentheses, having students finish the assignment at home, if necessary. Alternately, you may spend a period reading aloud a passage as a class, discussing the passage to check for comprehension, and then completing a short assignment based on the passage. At the end of a direct instruction unit on research techniques, you may have students write a report to demonstrate their learning. This is how writing has been taught for years.

In direct instruction, you teach, and students listen and learn. That being said, direct instruction is generally the least active form of learning, and too much reliance on this technique can lead to bored and unproductive students (Flowers, Hancock, & Joyner, 2000).

The Writing Workshop

According to Lucy McCormick Calkins (1986), "If students are going to become deeply invested in their writing, and if they are going to draft and revise, sharing their texts with each other as they write, they need the luxury of time" (p. 23). One format that allows this time, as well as a discovery-based approach to writing instruction, is the writing workshop. In this approach, teachers shift the focus from teaching to writing. However, a writing workshop also incorporates elements of direct instruction, using it to teach mini lessons during the first five to 15 minutes of class time. For the remainder of the time, students work on their own (authentic) writing projects, with an emphasis on the writing process.

Basically, a writing workshop consists of three components: (1) a 15-minute mini lesson; (2) approximately 20 minutes of independent student writing; and (3) 10 minutes of some form of sharing to wrap up the workshop. The beauty of a writing workshop is the emphasis it places on everyday writing and also the ability to free your time for small group instruction or even individual guidance, both of which are invaluable in differentiating your classroom to meet diverse needs (Ray, 2001).

As opposed to a direct-instruction classroom, a writing workshop relies less heavily on creative lesson design. As students will be spending the majority of their time involved in independent work, the goal of your mini lesson can be to teach one specific skill with high take-away value, and as it will be only 15 minutes long, you can ask students to remain focused even if your lesson is information-based.

A writing workshop depends on routine to create an environment of diligent and independent student work. As Calkins (1986) points out, "Setting aside predictable time for writing . . . allows children to take control of their own writing process" (p. 25). Workshop format also depends on well-planned scaffolding, in which you start with directed assignments and solid due dates and gradually release your control, moving toward authentic writing and making students accountable for a specific amount of portfolio work, but without project-by-project due dates.

Following is a usable assignment-by-assignment framework for starting and running a writing workshop.

Assignment 1

You choose the topic, for example, "About the Author," which also works well as a beginning-of-the-year ice-breaker. During your mini lesson, you model one step of the writing process; during this time you can also explain the mechanics of your workshop and reinforce your classroom routine. During independent student work, students use the exact same technique to complete this step on their own. It is also a good time to circulate around the class to offer help and guidance as needed. At the end of each period, ask students to share ideas, difficulties, or brief sections of their writing (being especially aware of creating a positive reading experience). As speedy students finish, have them write for fun, complete an extra-credit assignment, become editing partners for peers, or read a book of their choice. At the end of the assignment, the class reads their papers aloud in the format of an Author's Chair (discussed in depth on page 29).

Assignment 2

Again, you direct the topic. For example, you may choose to have students write about their personal hero. You model the prewrite and the draft, allowing students to complete the rest of the writing process with minimal prompting. Students finish at a defined due date, and you close the project with time set aside for Author's Chair.

Assignment 3

You start to release your topic constraints by asking the students to write a piece of descriptive writing about a topic they know well. You ask students to preview their topic and prewriting with you before drafting and offer small group and individual help as needed. During this time, your mini lessons are drawn from key curriculum components rather than spent reinforcing the mechanics of the writing process. You still ask for a traditional due date and close with Author's Chair.

Assignment 4

Before beginning this next assignment, you ask students to brainstorm a list of possible topics, perhaps in the form of "I will write to _____ about _____ so that _____." For example, "I will write to my school principal about skateboarding so that he/she will allow skateboards on the playground." Once students have listed many possible topics, allow them to choose their next writing assignment. At this point, you have the choice of releasing traditional due dates in favor of simply requiring a certain number of portfolio materials by the end of term, or you may choose to release only topic requirements and, for now, keep due dates (depending on the first few workshop assignments and the ability of your class). Releasing due dates has the advantage of little downtime for early finishers, as they will be able to start their next projects without waiting for the class to catch up. Releasing due dates also allows you to end many periods with an Author's Chair or two, rather than doing them all at once. It also allows a steady stream of assignments ready for assessment rather than the traditional pile.

Adding Components to the Writing Workshop

The Writing Workshop is a basic structure into which you can place many different components. However, as stated before, your workshop depends on routine, which can be hurt by the on-the-fly addition of components that break the daily classroom flow. Beware of adding anything until you have successfully created a routine with the elements you already use.

At first, you may simply ask students to transition successfully between the mini lesson, independent work, and sharing. As you add elements, be sure to prepare students in advance and then place these elements firmly into a weekly schedule so that students know, for example, that every Friday they will be responsible for Authentic Spelling instead of journaling. Make sure you retain a focus on the basic workshop framework and on students writing independently for the majority of the period, rather than overly compartmentalizing your instruction into an ongoing list of components. With that in mind, you will want to choose consciously and sparingly from the following list.

While the components below are described in the context of a writing workshop, you could easily transform many of them for use with direct instruction. Consider adding any or all of the following components to the structure of your writing workshop (each is described on the following pages):

- Author's Chair
- Journal Writing
- Assignment Packets
- Peer Revision
- Authentic Spelling
- Authentic Writing

Author's Chair

Author's Chair is an activity during which students share their published work aloud with the class—it is the culmination of the writing process and the point during which students will show off the product they have worked so hard on. It can also be terrifying! Thus, prior to your first Author's Chair, you will need to create a supportive classroom environment in which students feel comfortable sharing their work.

One way to do this is to encourage students to read short pieces or excerpts from longer works before jumping into a full-blown Author's Chair. Looking over a student's shoulder, you may notice an especially vivid sentence or paragraph in his/her writing; ask this student to read his or her work aloud as a model during the sharing/wrap-up portion of your writing workshop. If you can, make sure that every student gets a chance to read at least once during the first unit's writing process. And when they do, praise them highly. You will quickly know which students need a little extra support and which love to be in the spotlight. While the latter may ask if they can read aloud every day, your time is better spent bolstering your hidden introverts. Make sure that the class claps for each presenter, and always elicit three comments from students about what they liked in the piece. Save constructive criticism for elsewhere in the writing process.

In Author's Chair itself, make sure you create a clean distinction between this time and the rest of your writing workshop. Students should not be working while their classmates are reading aloud. Ask students to clear their desks of all distracting materials (i.e., everything) and to give their full attention to the reader. Again, students should clap at the end of each presentation and offer compliments.

The decision whether or not to force students into Author's Chair is up to you and can be made on a case-by-case basis. In the real world, writing can be shared from a distance, and many writers have been known to prefer the solitary approach, such as Ralph Waldo Emerson, Rick Bass, Annie Dillard, and Edward Abbey, to name a few. However, an audience is still a necessary element for writers. If students are unwilling to read their work aloud, you may offer to read it for them, but the experience of reaching an audience with their writing remains important.

During your first few assignments in which students will be finishing projects at or near the same date, you might schedule a few days specifically for Authors' Chairs. In later projects, you may have one or two students finishing a project every few days, and you can use the last couple of minutes of almost every period for the few Authors' Chairs that trickle in.

Journal Writing

At the beginning of each period, students may write in their journals about the day's prompt, or they may freewrite. As students enter the class, encourage them to find their writing folder and to have a seat. You may also ask that students not enter the room until they are ready to start work—allow students the extent of their valuable break, but ask that they leave their break behavior and noise level outside. On the board, you will have written the day's writing prompt. Students will use the sections of their notebooks dedicated to journaling to write their thoughts (either freely or based on the prompt). Let them know that writing journals are for their eyes only. Content in the journals will never be graded, although they may earn points for journaling a certain amount every day. Students may also use their journals to keep track of ideas for use in their larger assignments or with small group instruction if they have no draft in progress (Barlow, 2001).

Assignment Packets

For each major assignment, you may ask that students turn in not only their published work but also evidence of each step of the writing process. Students will staple into a packet their prewrite, draft, evidence of revision, evidence of editing, any required parent/teacher suggestions, and finally their published work, with a cover sheet that makes assessment easy. Collecting an assignment packet encourages a thorough use of the writing process, as well as the responsibility and organizational skills necessary to turn in a packet of materials.

Peer Revision

Many teachers and practitioners have begun to emphasize writing conferences as more productive means of providing an attentive, helpful audience (Freedman, Dyson, Flower, & Chafe, 1987). Peer revision not only benefits the author; rather, both students will gain from collaborating on the process of revision as they work to discover what makes writing *better* (Hughes, 1991). It is through this process of discovery and revision that students learn the tips and tricks they will use when drafting their next assignment. For example, during revision, students may focus on creating more precise word choice, so when they draft again, they will be more aware of their word choice and will have a clearer idea of what constitutes better word choice.

However, in peer revision, students will need to learn both the language and the tact of constructive criticism, as well as your behavioral expectations for independent conferencing . As Dyson and Freedman (1990) point out, "If peer group values conflict with classroom values, children may reject academic demands" (p. 9). Consider delegating authority, establishing a clear system of norms for behavior within the working groups, and monitoring closely the outcomes through increased teacher/student communications (Cohen, Intili, & Robbins, 1979). In terms of the mechanics of peer revisions, you might ask students to offer three compliments before adding two ideas for improvement (this avoids excessive back-patting as well as graceless criticism). Also, consider rewarding specific language (drawn from the Writing Process, the Traits of Good Writing, or your lessons) or especially insightful comments with a classroom reward of your choice. During the first few lessons and perhaps even beyond (judging based on the ability of your class), you may ask students to focus on only one area for peer revision, such as word choice, sentence fluency, ideas, voice, etc. (these are drawn from the Traits of Good Writing, which we will discuss in depth later). Reinforce the importance of peer group sharing as a tool that students will use to make their writing better.

Authentic Spelling

In Authentic Spelling, students use misspelled words from their own writing to create individualized spelling lists. These lists are then tested weekly, as in a traditional spelling program. Authentic Spelling is a strong tool for differentiating spelling lists to fit the widely varying levels of your students (Bartch, 1992). If you use Authentic Spelling in a writing workshop, it will take the place of journal writing on the day used (create a routine and note it on your Daily Information Board, as shown in Figure 1.1 on page 17).

According to Guy LeFrancois in his book *Psychology for Teaching* (2000), information is best committed to long-term memory if it is "personal and has organization that groups it to related material . . . material not brought to mind frequently enough (not used) tends to fade from memory" (p. 181). By learning to correctly spell words in their own writing, students will reinforce proper spelling with every assignment. A student's writing lexicon is personal, related to what he/she knows and uses with every piece of writing.

During the editing process, students, peers, parents, or the teacher will underline misspelled words (red pencil is useful). Once a week, students will look through their writing and list five of these underlined words on a note card. When listing, students may look up words in a dictionary to ensure the note card version is spelled correctly. Keep these note cards organized in a box and make this box accessible to students (after a few weeks, students should expect Authentic Spelling every day and should complete this entire process efficiently and independently).

On the same day that students create the note cards, have them find the prior week's note card and exchange it with a partner, who will then quiz the student on these five words (students write words on scrap paper as in a traditional spelling test). When finished, the partner scores the spelling test, and the partners exchange jobs. Once finished, students turn in their tests to the teacher for quick notation in the grade book. If you like, you can have students note their Authentic Spelling words in a designated section of their writing journals, allowing you to create monthly or yearly lists of words for which they are accountable (these lists can even follow them year to year).

Authentic Writing

In Authentic Writing, students choose their own topics, with a variety of guidance levels (some prompts, some open topics). For example, in the course of one period, you may have a student writing a persuasive piece about global warming, another writing a narrative about killer space monkeys, and another writing a letter to his/her grandmother. As Hudson (1988) illustrates, the more students control the form and content of their writing, the more likely they may be to perceive even assigned writing as their own.

However, without directed topics, you will undoubtedly encounter students who have difficulties brainstorming anything to write about. Before you can count on students to write authentically, you will need to scaffold them into the process. Be especially sure to teach many lessons on brainstorming and the elements that make a usable topic (i.e., the subject should be narrow and personal). In addition, you might ask students to keep an ongoing list of ideas in a writing journal. If they are ever stymied when searching for a topic, they can always reflect on their journals. Another useful strategy is to use a mini lesson to brainstorm topics as a class and allow students to write down their ten favorite topics for potential use later on.

If a student-chosen topic is the right hand of Authentic Writing, then real-world purpose is its left. In their book *On Teaching Writing*, Dyson and Freedman (1990) write, "Indeed, in the lives of children . . . literacy prospers if and when compelling reasons exist for writing . . ." (p. 4). This purpose can be as simple as the above-mentioned card to a grandmother or as complex as explaining a local environmental issue to government officials. By removing the stigma of purposeless busywork from writing assignments, you provide a clear reason for student work. And by allowing students to choose their own topics, you ensure that students will be interested in their writing.

Whatever the product, it is important in Authentic Writing for students to see their work take flight in the world. Publishing is an integral part of the process—if a student writes to a local official, make sure you actually send the letter; if a student writes an expository magazine article, submit it for publication. Even a rejection letter shows that someone read it!

Page 36 lists places where students can publish their writing. Figure 2.1 on page 37 shows a sample parent permission slip for publishing student work. You will also want to make your administrators aware of the fact that you intend to submit your students' work to publications.

Magazines That Publish Student Writing

There are local, regional, and national magazines that publish student writing. Some are listed below. Be sure to check in your area for other outlets.

Name of Company/Publication	Address	Notes
The Perfection Form Company	1000 North Second Ave. Logan, IA 51546 **http://www.perfectionlearning.com**	Will accept nonfiction and fiction
The Flying Pencil Press	P.O. Box 7667 Elgin, IL 60121	Will accept original writing and artwork from students ages 8–14
Cricket League	P.O. Box 300 Peru, IL 62354 **http://www.cricketmag.com**	Will accept original writing and artwork under an assigned theme or topic from students ages 5–9, 10–14, or 15–adult
Stone Soup	P.O. Box 83 Santa Cruz, CA 95063 **http://www.stonesoup.com**	Will accept original writing and artwork from students through age 13
Highlights for Children	803 Church Street Honesdale, PA 18431 **http://www.highlights.com**	Will accept original stories, articles, and craft ideas
Landmark Editions	Contest for Students 1904 Foxridge Dr. Kansas City, KS 66106 **http://www.landmarkeditions.com**	Have an annual "Written and Illustrated By" contest for students; will accept original written and illustrated stories

Figure 2.1: Sample Parent Permission Slip for Student Publishing

Dear Parents,

As part of our writing curriculum this year, we will be publishing student work in a variety of formats, including in print around school and potentially in other printed sources such as magazines, newsletters, and newspapers. At no time will we compromise your child's privacy. When publishing, your child's safety is our primary concern.

Sincerely,

Mr. Smith

- -

My son/daughter _____ has permission to publish his/her work in the course of the standard writing curriculum.

Parent Signature: _____

Direct Instruction and the Workshop

Many teachers feel there is simply too much required instruction to allow donating the majority of each period to independent work. Discovery-based learning might take a bit longer than direct instruction and, if your time is tight, you may need to compromise. However, the workshop and direct instruction need not be mutually exclusive. We have already looked at the role of direct instruction within the workshop as mini lessons, but if necessary, you can move your classroom framework another step toward an emphasis on direct instruction by using some days for workshop and others for lecture-format teaching.

However, alternating workshop days with lecture days is not recommended. In this model, students will have difficulties settling into the routine of independent work time, and you will need to police this time rather than use it for additional differentiated instruction (and thus defeating one main purpose in using the workshop). Students may also forget where in the writing process they are working and may need additional prompting to continue the train of their Authentic Writing thought. Instead, you may consider using direct instruction for however many weeks necessary before switching to the workshop format, using direct instruction to complete necessary curriculum elements and as a "warm up" to Authentic Writing. This approach has the advantage of making the workshop seem special to students.

Many teachers will also take a break from their full-time workshop for units on grammar or other strictly assessed issues (with this break just before the relevant assessment). Keep in mind, though, the danger of overly diluting the routine of your workshop, on which you will depend for a smoothly operating system.

Writing Topics

Directions: Write at least ten specific purposes for writing (such as "to inform my grandparent" or "to convince somebody of something") and topics in which you think students will be interested (such as "my best friend" or "what I want to be when I grow up"). When students get stuck, reference this list.

_____

_____

_____

_____

_____

_____

_____

_____

_____

_____

_____

_____

_____

_____

_____

_____

_____

_____

_____

Chapter 2 Reflection

1. How will you use your time in an average writing period?

   _____

   _____

   _____

2. Take a minute to reflect on your feelings about the Writing Workshop in comparison with direct instruction. What components of the Writing Workshop will you use in your classroom (even if you choose not to use the workshop)?

   _____

   _____

   _____

3. How will you use direct instruction in your classroom (even if you choose to use the workshop)?

   _____

   _____

   _____

4. How does your use of classroom time affect your physical classroom setup?

   _____

   _____

   _____

The Writing Process

In short, the writing process comprises the mechanics by which writers create publishable products. It is the method all writers use to generate ideas, choose and organize these ideas, write and revise their pieces, and format them for publication. In terms of instruction, it represents a holistic approach, encouraging creation of an entire product, rather than working on pieces of this process and only infrequently putting it all together (a procedure all too frequently seen in textbooks). Writing process instruction is just that—process oriented—and encourages young writers to discover for themselves the mechanics of composition. And while still infrequent in textbooks, Dyson and Freedman (1990) point out that over the past two decades, there has been a significant shift from a focus only on the products of writing to studying the processes associated with how writers write.

If you format your class as a writing workshop, the writing process will be indispensable, as it will be how students engage themselves for the majority of their time. Most questions that students have about what they should be working on can be answered by pointing to the next step of the writing process (consider posting the steps of the writing process as a wall chart). Simply put, your class periods could look like mini lessons, followed by student involvement in the writing process, and ending with a short discussion of the students' involvement with the writing process. This process is the end goal of writing instruction, is as close to real-world writing as is possible in the classroom, and will allow students to write for their own purposes in later life (outside the guidance of your lessons).

Of course, the pieces of the writing process differ depending on the type of writing being done (Morocco & Nelson, 1990). For example, in the prewrite phase of a research paper, you would likely include note cards and citations, whereas for a piece of narrative fiction, you might list a sequence of events and create a character list. In addition, the writing process will be slightly different for students with varying strengths and weaknesses. For example, one student may take pains to draft near-publishable writing while another may scribble ideas onto the page and then depend on the revision process to disentangle their thoughts.

In teaching the writing process, be aware that students will find their own methods. However, you will want to make sure that every student has a basis in and complete understanding of the basic steps, which they will need to use in some form (and which you may require to be turned in as part of an assignment packet). At least toward the beginning of the year, encourage students to use the following strategies:

- Prewriting
- Drafting
- Self Revising
- Peer/Adult Revising
- Editing
- Publishing

Prewriting

During prewriting, the first step of the writing process, authors will generate ideas and put their thoughts in order. Researchers such as Matsuhashi (1981) have found that as writing tasks become more complex and as more abstract thought is required, so too do experienced writers require more time to plan their writing. Examples of prewriting include anything from a sentence or two describing a project's organization to an extensive outline with references to where you will place notes. Three usable formats for prewriting include the following:

- Bubbling (mind web)

- Outlining

- Drawing/writing a captioned cartoon strip

Included here are sample templates for these three methods. You may want to provide students with templates at first, although once students are comfortable with the process, you may choose to let them prewrite without using templates. Depending on the level of flexibility your class can handle, you may decide to use these prewriting templates in one of the following ways:

- Distribute the appropriate template for every assignment.

- Scaffold the prewriting experience by distributing templates only for the first few assignments.

- Allow students to choose the prewriting form that works best for them.

- Distribute prewriting templates only for research assignments or longer works that require significant organizational skills.

- Teach the prewriting method appropriate to the assignment and distribute templates only to students who struggle.

- Choose not to use the sheets and support struggling students with individual or small group lessons.

Bubbling

Many authors refer to this technique as a mind web. Writing their topic in the center of the page, students will circle it and connect related ideas like cartoon quote bubbles. Students may turn in a sheet similar to the example on page 47 with their finished assignment packet or something more simple, like the template on page 48, depending on how many details they include.

From the central topic, the ideas connected directly to it may represent paragraphs in a draft, and the bubbles connected to these will likely become ideas that support the paragraph. By working toward higher levels of specificity as the bubbles extend from the center, students will create a logical path of thought and will have premade topic sentences supported with details.

Notice also that ideas can be interconnected. Using arrows, students can link two far-apart ideas. Perhaps in their draft, one of these ideas will be the last sentence of a paragraph, and the idea connected by an arrow will form the first sentence of the next, creating a logical flow between paragraphs.

Also, if a peripheral idea elicits a storm of connected thoughts, students may start a new prewriting sheet with this idea as their central bubble. For example, "jealous 'cause I couldn't catch anything" threatened to spin out of control in the example on page 47. Perhaps this could be a topic of its own on a new prewrite page.

If students get stuck, encourage them to dive into adjectives to explain one of their ideas more fully. For example, "grouper" could be connected to "spotted," "short-

and-fat," "huge mouth!" "bulging eyes," and "fins flap-ping." Using adjectives to picture their ideas, students will reconnect with their scene, setting, and story, and can push through moments of prewriting hesitation.

If students find thoughts popping up that don't necessar-ily flow from the preceding ideas, ask them to list these new ideas on the side and worry about bubbling them into the framework later.

The bubbling technique is generally the easiest of the three methods in which to brainstorm many ideas. However, it is also the least strict form of organizing these thoughts. Be sure to demonstrate how bubbles can become paragraphs.

Outlining

Outlining is the most directed and specific of the three methods of prewriting. In outlining, students describe the function and contents of each paragraph of their writ-ing by organizing ideas into topic sentences and support-ing details. While the included template on page 50 guides outlining for the standard five-paragraph paper, you can encourage students to apply the same ideas to longer papers (adding paragraphs) or to single-paragraph papers (by asking for only a main idea and supporting details). The included template is also most easily used with nonfiction writing in which students write a point-by-point description for the purpose of expository, per-suasive, or descriptive writing. Although this template can be used with narrative writing (fiction or nonfiction), it also has the ability to detract from the flow of a story by encouraging it to be overly sectionalized (as opposed to bubbling or the cartoon strip, which helps students organize a logical flow of "happenings").

Once a student organizes his/her ideas in outline form, he/she is likely to have few difficulties moving to a usable draft in paragraph form. However, drafts from a strict outline have the tendency, at first, to sound like a grocery list, with little flow. Notice that in the example outline (page 49), the student has listed only main ideas and details for three of the possible four paragraphs. When using this template, you can ask students to write a paper of a certain length or ask them to use the number of paragraphs they feel they need (even adding additional paragraphs to the outline sheet, if necessary).

Cartoon Strip

Especially in the early grades and for students with emergent organizational skills, prewriting in the form of a picture-by-picture comic strip can be useful (Harrington, 1994). Not only will students define the flow of events in their piece, but they may also be motivated by enjoying the process. This technique is especially appropriate for narrative/fiction writing.

Encourage students to avoid getting caught up in the artwork—while they will be using drawings, these drawings are for the purpose of organizing writing, not an end unto themselves. Have students caption their work in a way that describes the scenes, as shown in the sample cartoon strip on page 51. Page 52 has a basic template to use with your students.

Bubbling Example

Topic: _____   Audience: _____

Purpose: _____

```
  Four people
  to haul it          250 Pounds              Sightseeing              Humorous!
    aboard                                       Cruise

                   Grouper                                           "Teaching" little
                                                                     bro how to fish

        Ugly!                                    Australia           Big brother/little
                                                                          brother

  Bait with
corn/hotdogs               My Brother's                 Jealous 'cause          Rivalry
                            Big Fish                     I couldn't
                                                        catch anything
        Dropline

                                              Thought it was a
  Kite Spool               Offered to         snag on the reef
                            cut line

                                                              Until it moved

            Running out
             of string
                                                              Fought two hours

                     Could have
                      lost It                          Didn't want
                                                       Dad's help
```

Excerpted from *Implementing an Effective Writing Program* by Kristi Pikiewicz and Garth Sundem. Copyright ©2004 by Shell Education.

Bubbling Template

Topic: _____   Audience: _____

Purpose: _____

Use the space below to "bubble" your ideas.

Write your main idea in the center of the page, circle it, and connect other idea bubbles to it with lines.

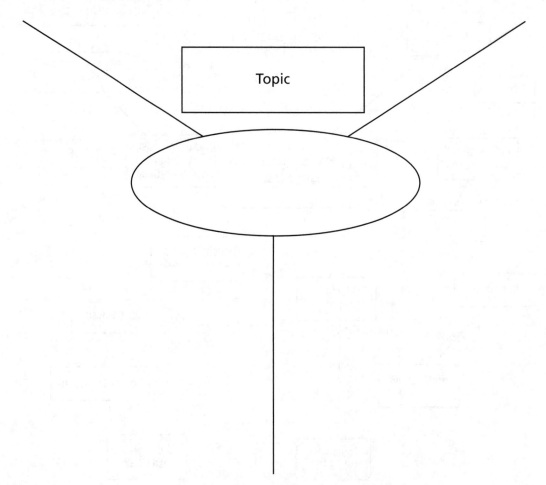

Excerpted from *Implementing an Effective Writing Program* by Kristi Pikiewicz and Garth Sundem. Copyright ©2004 by Shell Education.

Outline Example

Name: Joe Student   Date: _____

1. **The goal of my paper is to** tell readers about Thomas Jefferson and the challenges
   he faced as president.

2. **Describe the type of person who will read your writing (your audience):**
   Hopefully, kids my age who read *Cricket Magazine* (because when I'm done, I will
   submit it).

3. **List three details you will use in your introduction to interest readers:**
   Detail: Thomas Jefferson was a slave owner but also believed that "all men are
   created equal."
   Detail: He made the Louisiana Purchase, which more than doubled the size of the
   United States.
   Detail: His enemy, Alexander Hamilton, actually *helped* to get him elected.

4. **List the main idea of each paragraph and the details/facts that go with it.**
   Main Idea: He had to decide what to do about settlers and Native Americans.
   Detail: Settlers "owned" land—a concept that was foreign to Native Americans.
   Detail: Jefferson forced Native American tribes to move west of the Mississippi.
   Detail: He thought there was so much space out west that tribes would live in
   peace.
   Main Idea: The Louisiana Purchase
   Detail: The French offered to sell us a huge amount of land, because they needed
   money.
   Detail: The U.S. was already growing so big that we needed the land.
   Detail: Jefferson had to choose whether to follow the law or to quickly make the
   purchase.
   Main Idea: The election of 1800
   Detail: There was a tie between Jefferson and Aaron Burr.
   Detail: Alexander Hamilton, who agreed with Aaron Burr but didn't like him,
   helped break the tie in Jefferson's favor.
   Detail: Burr was so mad that he challenged Hamilton to a duel and shot him!
   Main Idea: _____
   Detail: _____
   Detail: _____
   Detail: _____

5. **List one detail that you will use in your conclusion to make readers think.**
   In Jefferson's time, there was still a chance we would be taken over by some other
   country. How do you think this affected his decisions?

Outline Template

Name: _____ Date: _____

1. **The goal of my paper is to** _____
   _____

2. **Describe the type of person who will read your writing (your audience):**
   _____
   _____

3. **List three details you will use in your introduction to interest readers:**
   Detail: _____
   Detail: _____
   Detail: _____

4. **List the main idea of each paragraph and the details/facts that go with it.**
   Main Idea: _____
   Detail: _____
   Detail: _____
   Detail: _____
   Main Idea: _____
   Detail: _____
   Detail: _____
   Detail: _____
   Main Idea: _____
   Detail: _____
   Detail: _____
   Detail: _____
   Main Idea: _____
   Detail: _____
   Detail: _____
   Detail: _____

5. **List one detail that you will use in your conclusion to make readers think.**
   _____
   _____

Cartoon Strip Example

Topic: _____ Audience: _____

Purpose: _____

We get up in the morning and get ready for work.	The dog looks nice and well behaved.	We go out the door and wave goodbye.	The dog sleeps until he's sure that we're gone.

He gets up and looks around with a mischievous look on his face.	Out the window he goes with all our shoes!	We come home from work.	The dog is sleeping and pretends he knows nothing about the shoes.

Excerpted from *Implementing an Effective Writing Program* by Kristi Pikiewicz and Garth Sundem. Copyright ©2004 by Shell Education.

Cartoon Strip Template

Topic: _____ Audience:_____

Purpose:_____

Use the space below to draw a cartoon strip of your ideas. Make sure to write what is happening under your pictures.

Pictures				
Captions (words)				

Pictures				
Captions (words)				

Excerpted from *Implementing an Effective Writing Program* by Kristi Pikiewicz and Garth Sundem. Copyright ©2004 by Shell Education.

Drafting

Each use of the writing process is likely to take most students a similar amount of time, although the steps on which they spend their time may vary. For example, if students spend time on their prewriting, they will gain it back while drafting; if they rush through the prewrite, they may take longer to draft. This is to be expected. Some students will fly through the planning stage of their writing, giving it the minimum required effort and nimbly inserting ideas on the fly as they draft. Others will agonize over their prewrite and view the draft as "filling in the blanks" of an organized outline. Both approaches have their advantages and disadvantages.

Regardless of the prewriting approach that leads into drafting, you will want students to keep the following in mind:

• *Drafting Need Not Be Perfect Writing*

Many students will focus on the fact that their draft doesn't sound published as it flows off their pen. They know that words are misspelled, certain things could have been better said, and maybe the punctuation is sketchy at best, and they won't be able to continue until they "fix" the problem. While some drafters may simply be perfectionists, the majority of writers fear exposing a perceived lack of writing ability. The most powerful thing you can do to hearten timid drafters is to share your own drafts and model the revision necessary to turn drafts into publishable work. This is also important in showing that revision is necessary—an important point for students who feel that their first draft must be a finished product. When doing this, make sure your draft sounds choppy—you also need to be comfortable sharing in-process work in front of the class. By sharing a rough draft with students, you will show them it's all right to struggle in their first attempts. By demonstrating that strong language can be culled from a choppy draft, you will keep students from despairing when their drafts sound less than perfect.

• *Drafting Is Cyclical*

Although you should encourage students to write a draft based on the information from their prewrite, they need not be completely bound by it. While drafting, encourage students to revise as little as possible, but if they have additional good ideas, they can brainstorm, organize, and revise to a degree. Dahl and Farnan (1998) describe the various paths students take through the writing process as, ". . . not a straight superhighway from idea to finished text [but] more like a twisting mountain road with a lot of switchbacks" (p. 8). A prewrite is a valuable road map, but if students hit a traffic jam along the way, encourage them to be flexible in determining an alternate route. If later writing provokes an idea that fits earlier in the piece, have them insert the idea! At one extreme, a draft can end up looking like a more detailed prewrite, with notes in the margins, scribblings inserted above sentences, and whole passages crossed out and rewritten elsewhere; at the other end, a draft can be ready for print. Students will fan out along the spectrum according to their own needs as authors.

• *The Teacher's Role While Drafting*

As students are drafting, you will be giving individual and small group help as needed. However, be wary of distracting students in this step; what looks like "stuck" might actually be "deep in thought." Give encouragement, but not at the expense of breaking a student's concentration. As you circulate, also ask students if they would mind sharing interesting parts of their draft with the class toward the end of the period. Asking students to share can be a strong pat on the back. As a motivational tool, you may ask struggling students to share anything they manage to get down. By making them feel successful, you have helped them take a leap toward actual success.

Revising

Revising is often neglected in the writing process. Students often feel that they have already written the paper, and they see any extra work, such as revising, as just that—extra work. But in revising lies the greatest potential for learning. While revising, students learn techniques to make their writing better—techniques they can apply the next time they draft. Students will see "before" and "after" versions, and by comparing the two, they will demonstrate to themselves the specific elements that make for a better piece of writing (Adams, 1991). In this multistep process, it is effective for students to first revise their own work and then get comments from a peer or adult.

Keep in mind the following ideas when teaching students to revise their work:

• *Teach the Mechanics of Revision*

Generally, students have three options for demonstrating revision. They may mark directly on their draft, they may recopy onto a new page as they go, or they may first mark on their draft and then recopy it for legibility. The first method does away with much busywork, allowing students more time to focus on important elements of writing; however, when asking peers or adults to help revise their work, students will need a legible draft that can be easily read and that allows for a fluid reading. You will need to demonstrate these mechanics.

Also, before asking students to revise their work, teach the common revision/proofreading marks. The most important points are showing students how to add and delete material and demonstrating techniques they might not think of, such as actually cutting up their draft and pasting it back together to change large-scale organization. Not only will students be marking their own work, but they will eventually be revising others' work. Therefore, strive to teach them universal editing marks that can be understood by everyone.

• *Students Need Specifics*

"Children tend to overestimate their own and others' comprehension of text, and thus, they do not identify specific areas of text that could benefit from revision" (Beal, 1993, p. 643). At first, you may need to ask students to revise very specific elements (such as one of the Traits of Good Writing, as described in Chapter 4). Consider using mini lessons (in a writing workshop) to demonstrate revision of passages on an overhead. Once you have picked a revision topic, such as word choice, work as a class to revise the passage such that each student gains a picture of exactly what makes one word "better" than another. After demonstrating, ask students to apply the same technique in their own writing.

• *One Thing at a Time!*

Until students are proficient in noticing what needs revision, they should revise for only one issue at a time, likely one of the Traits of Good Writing. Perhaps on the first pass they will look only at their organization, and on the next they will evaluate their use of word choice, and so on. This will help students put specific language to their nagging idea that *something* isn't quite right. As many of the traits are interrelated (disturbing a piece's organization will affect sentence fluency), you may want to encourage students to revise in the following order: ideas, organization, word choice, voice, sentence fluency.

- *Make the Distinction Between Revising and Proofreading*

Revising is for content, while proofreading (editing) is for conventions (Reed, 1995). As long as the conventions used in a draft allow the material to be readable, your students will revise only for content in this step, rather than proofreading for spelling and grammar, which they will do while editing. To reinforce this important distinction, you may ask students to use a different color pencil for revision than for editing. For example, you may keep a class set of green pencils for use *only* while revising and a set of red pencils *only* for editing/proofreading.

Peer/Parent Revising

In Hillocks' (1984) extensive evaluation of writing instruction techniques, one of the few absolutes was his recommendation of small group collaboration on problem-solving activities related to writing. The goal of this collaboration between students (or indeed, between students and any reader) is the transfer of information from author to reader. For example, it may be obvious to the author that his/her dog attacking the postal carrier is a humorous situation, but if the author fails to adequately describe his/her eight-week-old Pomeranian puppy, the audience may miss the humor. Additionally, an author may have the intended cadence of a sentence in his/her mind, but through peer/parent revision may find that, without proper punctuation, the sentence is difficult to read. In both cases, the audience is the best barometer of success. Also, through working to revise someone else's writing, students will collaboratively learn techniques they can use in their own writing.

The adult/parent revision option allows you to involve parents more closely in their child's education and helps bridge the gap between school and home. You may require both peer and adult revision, offer the option of one or the other, or simply use peer revision, as this technique is easier to control in the format of your classroom and requires less organized correspondence.

Keep the following in mind when encouraging parent/peer revisions:

• Give Specifics

Just as revision by the writer needs to be focused, so does revision by an adult/peer. If comments become lengthy, students are likely to either have so much to apply that they don't know where to begin, or they misinterpret the number of comments as negative criticism. Consider guiding peer revisions such that partners look for only one aspect of writing during the revision process. With older or more able classes, you might encourage partners to take "multiple passes" through each other's writing, but still only focusing on one aspect of writing at a time. Again, this is a likely place to insert language from the Traits of Good Writing.

If you are using parent revision, you will likely want to create cover sheets that guide the revision. For example, you might explain how to detect problems with sentence fluency (i.e., *Read the paper aloud and notice where you stumble*); then ask parents to list three sentences they think are especially *good*, list two that could use revision, and finally offer suggestions for revision.

• All Parents Aren't Effective Teachers

Adults may need guidance and redirection, just as their children do. Since you have little chance to guide adults as they revise their child's work at home, you will likely want to communicate through revision cover sheets as described above. If you find that parents aren't performing effectively, you can either call to iron out the difficulties, encourage students to work with a different adult, or choose to use peer revision instead. Some parents will enjoy the ability to affect their child's education, while others may see parent revision as a stress on their time and part of a job that you, the teacher, should be taking care of. There is no need to make this into a battle; if parents choose to be uninvolved, you may decide to let them.

Another scenario is that in which parents are overly involved and untactful in their comments. The parents want to help but end up hurting their child's writing confidence. In this case, you will need to help them understand that progress takes time and that one specific comment goes much further toward improving their child's writing than does, "Thomas obviously doesn't know how to write. He needs to revise his piece again." If you find a version of this comment, the parent needs to know how hurtful it is to their child's writing.

• *Prepare Students to Give Each Other Comments*

Keep in mind that students will need both revision skills and tact in order to successfully peer-edit another student's writing. As discussed earlier in the Peer Revision section of the Writing Workshop, when modeling the process, you will want to show students how to give three positive comments for every two negative ones and help authors see that "negative" is actually "constructive"—this follows the widely-used format of *Praise-Question-Polish* (Neubert & McNelis, 1990). While you don't want students to come to blows or tears over another's comments, neither do you simply want a back-patting session in which students learn little about improvement. At first, you may want to create, distribute, and use revision cover sheets, just as you do to help guide parent revisions.

However, you will also want to encourage students to discuss their writing freely and to experiment with ideas to improve it. Through discussing revision options outside the framework of a guided sheet, students will have the chance to experiment with the literary vocabulary you have been teaching as well as taking ownership of their own learning.

• *Remember: Revision Is Not Proofreading*

Many adults' initial reaction to their student's writing is to correct it. In this step, encourage students and adults to look at the *content* of the piece rather than the conventions. Unless a student is significantly below grade level in his/her mastery of conventions, save proofreading for later.

• *Incorporating Revisions*

Once a student has adult/peer comments on how to improve his/her writing, he/she will choose which suggestions to incorporate in their draft. Simply knowing what they "could have done" is not enough—encourage students to actually *use* these revision comments to improve their writing. Again, revisions can be evidenced by scratchings and scribblings on the initial double-spaced draft, or they can take the form of a new copy (especially if using computers). That being said, simply because a revision is suggested does not mean that students must use it. As long as they can defend their choices, students may choose to use or not use revision ideas as they see fit. However, if a student chooses not to use a suggested revision, you may ask him/her to justify the decision in writing, thus removing the temptation to shirk revisions as a way of getting out of "extra" work. Your goal in this step is to ask students to be conscious of what makes, or could make, their writing better. Explaining an unused suggestion accomplishes this goal just as well as utilizing the suggestion.

Proofreading/Editing

The method for teaching conventions elicits one of the most heated debates in teaching. To drill or not to drill—that is the question. However, most teachers (and the majority of researchers) agree that an emphasis on context is helpful. Butyniec-Thomas & Woloshyn (1997) note that "young children learn to spell best when they are taught a repertoire of effective strategies in a meaningful context" (p. 294).

Authors who write without a command of conventions will have difficulty getting their work taken seriously. But are conventions the be-all and end-all of strong writing? Writers use conventions the way a carpenter uses a hammer—as a tool. Conventions are a way to express thoughts and feelings, but they are not the expression themselves. Content, creativity, and style create interest, but without conventions that interest can be buried in incredibility.

Editing as part of the writing process should first be done by the author and then again by a peer or adult, using the appropriate editing marks. Just as in revision, it is useful to ask students to make multiple "passes" through their writing, checking only one area at a time, for example spelling, paragraphing, or commas. Ask students to first read their pieces aloud to themselves (quietly), checking for hesitations or glitches, which can point to grammar or punctuation problems. Have students cross out and replace rather than erase, which quickly erodes a draft into smudge marks and holes. Remind students to be especially aware of the following grammar issues:

- **Punctuation**—Does each sentence end with the proper mark? Are phrases broken into sentences where appropriate? Are there run-ons or fragments? Are pauses marked by commas?

- **Capitalization**—Are beginnings of sentences, dates, and proper nouns capitalized?

- **Agreement**—Do sentences agree in number and tense?

- **Tense**—Is tense consistent throughout?

Be sure to ask peers/parents to *underline* misspelled words, as you will then be able to ask the author to use these words in creating Authentic Spelling lists (if you choose to use this technique). One useful trick is to ask students to use *green* pencils when revising and red pencils when editing. If your students realize that by finding misspellings, they are giving themselves Authentic Spelling work, they may choose to overlook their mistakes—you may need to give students a quota, asking them to underline at least five to ten words. Even if a word is spelled correctly, simply being unsure is enough to warrant its inclusion on an Authentic Spelling list.

Once students have completed their own proofreading, ask them to either trade papers with a classmate or to use an adult editing partner. The peer/adult editor will mark the draft in the same way as did the author. At the end of proofreading, students should have a draft with the exact words and organization that will be in their published copy. It should be covered in red pencil with notes and generally look like it's been through the washing machine, which in a way it has. Scrubbed clean of errors and sparkling with style, your students' writing is ready for publishing.

Publishing

Like attention to conventions, the neatness and presentation of a piece of writing will help ensure that readers take it seriously. The next great American novel will languish on the shelf if it isn't presented in a way that makes readers peek at the dust jacket. A business proposal detailing the next revolution in nanotechnology won't be taken seriously if scrawled in pencil on the back of a napkin. Granted, presentation has nothing to do with content, but in the writing process, and to allow students to use writing for their own purposes later in life, they will need to learn how to present their work appropriately.

Additionally, publishing is central to the implementation of Authentic Writing (as discussed in Chapter 2), which, you will remember, includes the pairing of choice and purpose. How and where you publish student writing will determine whether it in fact has purpose or whether the writing was simply an exercise. The writing workshop format, and thus your writing-process class, is helped greatly by intrinsic motivation. Publishing student writing as part of a class magazine, in the school newsletter, or potentially even in a local or national magazine can be a powerful motivation for students to turn in their best work (Weber, 2002).

The obvious publishing task is for students to rewrite their drafts, preferably on a computer (unless they can justify writing in pen, as would be appropriate for a personal note to their grandmother). You will likely want to create class publishing norms, which you can solidify with class input—ask your students what they think should be standard publishing procedure and then have them make an informational poster to be hung in your classroom.

Below are ideas for publishing student work with purpose:

- Hang published work around your classroom—make sure students write a large, eye-catching title and perhaps have them mount their writing on an artistic background. This works especially well for short pieces that can be published on one or two pages and thus don't require page turns.

- Publish in the school or PTA newsletter.
- Create a class magazine.
- Submit to the local newspaper.
- Submit to local or national magazines.
- Write letters to personalities or policy makers.
- Create informative or entertaining posters to be hung around the school.
- Search out and submit work to writing contests.
- Find pen or e-mail pals in other countries.
- Create a class website.
- Share with other classes or grades.
- Create a writing share with another school.

Scaffolding the Writing Process

If you simply ask students to use the writing process and then leave them to their own devices, you will quickly find yourself confronted with a room full of confused pupils. While you eventually want students to complete the writing process independently, you will need to scaffold your instruction toward this goal (as discussed earlier in the section on Authentic Writing).

One successful technique is to first model the procedure, then ask students to share their writing with you, and finally to support students as they attempt the writing on their own (Boyle & Peregoy, 1990). In the format of the writing process, this may look like demonstrating how to fill in a mind web as you prewrite a piece of writing. Next, you may ask students to suggest a topic, brainstorm ideas as a class, and then have students organize these ideas into a mind web. Finally, you could ask the students to perform the same procedure individually, prewriting the topic of their first assignment.

You can apply this same teaching technique to each step of the writing process, modeling, sharing, and then asking for independent completion. At first, you will want to teach a step and have students follow this instruction by completing the same step on their own, working at a similar pace through the writing process. As discussed in Authentic Writing, once students are comfortable with each step, they may spread out across the process, choosing to spend varying amounts of in-class time on each step.

Chapter 3 Reflection

1. What is the role of the writing process within a writing workshop?

   _____

   _____

   _____

   _____

2. How does the writing process encourage real-world writing and students' abilities to write for their own purposes in later life?

   _____

   _____

   _____

3. Where and how will you use the writing process in your classroom?

   _____

   _____

   _____

   _____

4. How will you scaffold your students' use of the writing process?

   _____

   _____

   _____

Assessment and the Traits of Good Writing

Assessment and accountability are more important than ever in education, and whatever the assessment strategy you use in your writing class, you will no doubt need to justify your methods to parents, administrators, and/or other teachers. Make sure to clear any deviations from district and school policy before implementing your own assessment strategy. In addition, regardless of the assessment strategy you use on a day-to-day basis, you will want to be sure to at least preview the assessment that is used on your district examinations.

As you read this chapter, keep in mind that assessment is not grading (a similar comparison to revision and editing). In assessment, you will try to pinpoint your students' areas of strength and weakness for use in assessment-driven, differentiated instruction. Grading is mentioned only in a few places and refers to the numbers you will put on a report card. Of course, assessment is frequently a step on the path to grading. If, for example, a student demonstrates a significant deficiency in one aspect of writing, you may not need to assign this deficiency a specific number. Rather, you will be content in assessing this student's area of instructional need, which you will then target with directed lessons. In most classrooms, grading remains a tried-and-true method for communicating overall performance, but you will need to be more specific for the purposes of instruction.

Trait-Based Assessment

Many states have now adopted trait-based assessment. In fact, Suzie Boss (2002), writing for the Northwest Regional Labs notes that, "the trait framework has spread . . . to every state and to many countries around the world" (para. 5). Dahl and Farnan (1998) write that, "As an assessment system, [trait-based assessment] offers information that can best assist instruction because each element in a writing is evaluated separately, with each characteristic marked on a scale that indicates how well it has been presented" (p. 113).

The Traits of Good Writing is basically a rubric for assessing writing, although you may also use the traits for instruction and discussion. In this method, teachers separate writing into its components of Voice, Organization, Sentence Fluency, Ideas, Word Choice, Conventions, and sometimes Presentation, scoring each trait from 1 to 5 (or 1–4 or 1–6, depending on your district). Trait-based assessment allows an objective measure of writing, while helping you to pinpoint the areas where each student could improve (Steineger, 1996). In addition, by scoring each trait independently of the others, you may also give students positive feedback on their areas of strength (Isernhagen & Kozisek, 2000).

Much like the strategy you will encourage in peer editing of offering three positive comments to every two ideas for improvement, the Traits of Good Writing allow you to make students feel good about their writing, while continuing to target areas of weakness with differentiated lessons. You can also use the traits as the vocabulary for discussing what makes writing "good" or "bad," be it students' own writing or published work. For example, you might use lesson time to read a newspaper article and discuss its use of organization or sentence fluency. By raising awareness of each of these traits, students will learn to recognize them in their own writing and will have specifics for use in gauging and improving the quality of their work.

However, the Traits of Good Writing take some getting used to. At first, you may find this type of assessment cumbersome and time-consuming. Luckily, there are many time-saving tricks, and your per-paper time will improve dramatically as you get more comfortable with the traits themselves. If your district does not currently use the traits for grading, consider using trait-based assessment with certain students in order to pinpoint areas of deficiency for targeted lessons.

Other Assessment Strategies

In addition to trait-based assessment, which will be covered in great detail in this chapter, you may also consider the following three assessment strategies as needed.

Holistic Assessment

Holistic assessment refers to an overall impression based on a student's writing performance when compared with that of the rest of the class. In their book *Children's Writing*, Dahl and Farnan (1998) define holistic assessment as, "assessing writing based on a general impression, usually represented by a single score" (p. 113).

Teachers generally communicate holistic assessment with written comments that tend to be proportional to the length of the assignment. If you use this method, make sure to make notes about each student's skills for use in later lessons. In addition, you may choose to combine this holistic technique with a predefined number of points taken for conventions issues, such as misspelled words. Overall, the holistic assessment method is a highly traditional approach, although it lacks the framework for both creating an objective measure of performance and breaking this performance into its components for differentiating instruction.

Portfolio Assessment

Portfolio assessment is the process of collecting student work over a period of time and using it to make conclusions about overall performance (Wortham, Barbour, & Desjean-Perrotta, 1998). The method of assessing the assignments within the portfolio is up to you. Portfolio assessment works well with the outlined model for the writing workshop/writing process, as students should already be keeping assignments organized in their writing folders. If students release their writings into the world, such as letters to state representatives, magazine submissions, or notes to their grandparents, ask them to make a photocopy for inclusion in their portfolio.

This method has the advantage of making it easier to spot trends. Perhaps on an assignment-to-assignment basis, you would miss a student's lack of a concluding sentence (or paragraph); but in a portfolio, this will be a more obvious area for improvement as you notice that the lack of a conclusion is consistent. Depending on your school and district, you may be able to use portfolio assessment in place of traditional grading. If this is the case, you will likely be required to "boil down" a student's portfolio to areas of strength and weakness, which you can include on a cover sheet.

Assignment-Specific Rubrics

Especially in a content-driven assignment, such as a research report, book review, or retention-check, you can create an assignment-specific rubric to check for understanding (Rickards & Cheek, 1999). In this method, you would assign a certain number of points for various items you would like to see in the students' writing. For example, you could require that students describe at least three characters in the course of a book review and assign five points for each description.

There are many strategies for creating individualized rubrics, but in general you will want the rubric to match the purpose of your assignment as specifically as possible. For example, if you were creating a rubric to assess students' writing journals, you would likely prioritize a certain daily volume and de-emphasize, or do away with completely, checking for conventions. In this assignment, your purpose is to encourage students to write their thoughts on a daily basis, not to ensure that these thoughts are written in perfect prose.

Make sure you preview your rubrics with students so they have a clear picture of how they will be assessed. For longer assignments, you may even wish to send the rubric home with students to be signed by parents.

Whatever the rubric for a given assignment, make sure to keep track of not only the grade, but also areas in which individual students excel or need additional work. With a more style-driven assignment, such as a short story or description, you may have difficulties defining your parameters for performance in the format of a traditional rubric (other than specifying length or detracting for missed conventions, which likely misses the point of your assignment). For these assignments, consider adding written comments as you would in the holistic grading method or think about a different assessment strategy.

The Traits Defined

Ideas

Ideas make up the content of a piece. A main idea, or topic/story line, is supported by vivid and relevant accompanying details. Ideas interest and inform, excite and entertain; in good writing, they define a thought perfectly, while remaining unexpected, fresh, precise, and concise. Good ideas describe a situation without having to name it (show, don't tell).

Word Choice

The best word choice paints a picture that can be interpreted in no other way. Through attention to nuance, poetry, and connotation, authors pick words that in hindsight seem like the only possible choices. If the night is "hot," could it better be described as "sweltering," "languid," or "wet-skinned"? Word choice can also refer to content-specific vocabulary, which you may assess as part of a lesson.

Sentence Fluency

Sentence fluency creates musical text that yearns to be read aloud. Sentences flow without hesitation in varied and creative forms, creating an ever-changing rhythm. Logical connections bridge the gap between one sentence and the next, such that ideas seem to blend and evolve rather than stop and start.

Voice

A piece with strong voice could have been written by the author and no other. Personality jumps from the page, and the author's passion and interest in the topic is evident. The writing speaks directly to the intended audience, creating a connection between reader and author.

Organization

The piece is constructed in a way that leads from an interesting opening to a thought-provoking conclusion without unnecessary digression. While pieces need not be predictable, they have a logical framework, showing care in planning and foresight. Details are relevant to the section in which they are included and combine to support the topic or story line.

Conventions

Does the student demonstrate a mastery of grade-appropriate grammar, punctuation, spelling, paragraphing, capitalization, etc.? Anything included in the mechanics of language falls into the category of conventions.

Presentation

Strong presentation offers information in a manner that is visually appealing and clear. Meaning is highlighted by layout, graphics, and neatness, and readers are immediately drawn to give the piece a closer look.

Scoring the Traits

In trait-based assessment, most districts ask that you score each trait from 1 to 5 (5 is highest), although others prefer a 1–4 or a 1–6 scale. You will score each trait independently to find exactly where a student needs work and where he/she is proficient. Thus, the highest score for a standard assignment using the Traits of Good Writing is 35 (seven traits, times the possible score of 5). This total score describes a student's overall writing ability.

While the rubric included with this book uses a 1–5 scale, you can easily use it in trait-based assessment on other scales, especially if your goal is assessment for the purposes of assessment-driven instruction. You can stop once you have found a student's weakness, no matter what the score is. During your first attempts at assessment using the Traits of Good Writing, you will want to keep the rubric close at hand, referencing it as needed. As you become more comfortable and are independent of the printed rubric, your assessment speed will increase dramatically.

Holistic Writing Trait Scoring Rubric

	5	3	1
Ideas	The paper's central idea is clear and focused and is supported by vivid, relevant details.	The writer has defined a topic, but it is supported by few or by mundane details.	The writer has not defined a topic; details are lacking or irrelevant.
Word Choice	The writer uses precise, natural, and engaging words to convey the intended message.	While the writer's meaning is clear, word choice lacks energy; words are functional but routine.	Words are used incorrectly or the writer uses such limited vocabulary that meaning is impaired.
Voice	The writer is obviously aware of the audience, communicating in an engaging and personal tone.	While functional, the voice is impersonal; the piece could have been written by anybody.	The writer seems indifferent to the audience or topic; readers are unmoved and left flat.
Sentence Fluency	Sentences flow easily and are a pleasure to read aloud.	The text is mechanical rather than musical.	The text can be read aloud only with practice. Many structural problems exist.
Organization	Organization supports the topic and moves the reader through the text cleanly.	Readers find meaning without undue confusion, but their path is indirect.	There is no identifiable structure. Events and information are random.
Conventions	Even complex conventions enhance meaning and readability. Errors are few.	The writer has control of the basic conventions but struggles to use anything more complex.	Errors make the piece difficult to read. The writer uses basic conventions incorrectly.
Presentation	Layout and presentation enhance meaning and visual appeal.	The piece is readable and neat, neither adding to nor detracting from meaning and appeal.	Presentation is distracting or messy, making meaning unclear.

Excerpted from *Implementing an Effective Writing Program* by Kristi Pikiewicz and Garth Sundem. Copyright ©2004 by Shell Education.

Practice Scoring

While using the seven traits to assess student writing sounds daunting at first, with practice the technique can actually prove less cumbersome than traditional grading. Like any skill, you will need to get a couple of attempts under your belt before it becomes comfortable. Included are a few example papers with discussion of why they earned the accompanying scores.

After exploring the examples, you may still want to attempt the assessment process outside of classroom pressure. The most useful practice technique is to recruit an assessment partner, possibly a colleague also interested in improving his/her use of the Traits of Good Writing. Pick student writing to study, and assess it independently. Once you have scored the writing without collaboration, compare your scores and discuss.

Don't worry if your scores do not match at first. This is a learning process in which you will both be exploring the nuances of the traits. Discussion of your disparities in scores is as important, if not more important, than coming to a consensus on what number each trait deserves. Neither of you will be "wrong," but by justifying your score, you will gain experience with the language of the traits and the issues that deserve certain scores.

As you read the following student work, jot down your scores and comments. After you have done your own assessment, flip to the suggested scores and comments. Presentation is not assessed, because layout and handwriting/font have been changed. Also, feel free to photocopy the examples for distribution among a team of seven-trait learners.

1. ALL ABOUT ME

Grade 5

Prompt: "About the Author"

Hi everyone! My name is Tommy Chadakar, and I'm here to tell you all about me. There are a lot of thing I've done in my life, and I'm sure you'll enjoy this. I've had an extremely interesting life so far.

I have a small inner family and a huge bunch of relatives. I live with my mother, father, and little sister in Novato, California. I have about twenty cousins, and twelve sets of aunts and uncles. I have many more relatives, but if I start listing them, I'll take up the whole page.

I come from a small but beautiful country call Sri Lanka. It is a small island, about thirty miles off the southern tip of India. It is about two hundred seventy miles north to south, and about one hundred forty miles east to west. This is where just about all my relatives live. Sri Lanka's population at last count was about eighteen million people, but there are probably a lot more people now.

This past summer must have been one of the best I've ever had. I was having so much fun I didn't notice how the time went by. First of all, I went to camp for one week. My buddies went with me, and we had great fun together. My favorite part was after dinner, when we played cards until about ten o'clock. After that my family drove to Los Angeles, where we picked up my relatives from the airport. The next day, we went to Disneyland and thoroughly enjoyed ourselves. After Disneyland, we went to Universal Studios. I loved the rides.

So, like I said, I've had an interesting life. It is packed with fun. I hope you enjoyed reading about me, and I'll tell you this. I like my life so much that I wouldn't trade it for anyone else's.

Ideas: _____ Organization: _____ Sentence Fluency: _____

Voice: _____ Word Choice: _____ Conventions: _____

2. MY PET

Grade 1

Prompt: "Describe a pet that you have or you wish you had"

My pet is a fish. His name is Fliper. We dont no if he is a boy or a girl. My sister thinks he is a girl. But I think he is a boy. My Mom and Dad dont no. Fliper dos not do much. He swims. He eats. He breeths. He looks arond the room. I wonder what he sees. I love Fliper.

Ideas: _____ Organization: _____ Sentence Fluency: _____

Voice: _____ Word Choice: _____ Conventions: _____

3. GWALYGALOOP:
Flyicus Backwardus

Grade 6

Prompt: "Describe a fictional animal"

This strange bird lives in the low plains area. Mainly, what is so strange about the gwalygaloop, is that it flies backward and is featherless. It also lays square eggs. Because of this, when they lay their eggs, they make a Oooooo, Ahhhhhh, sound. This distinguishing sound has given them the nickname OoAh bird. When the eggs hatch, the chicks come out with mature feathers. As they grow older, they trade in their feather for a leathery membrane connecting the wings like a bat. Now, comes the hard part. Flying is very tough for the gwalygaloop to learn because they must learn to fly backwards. This can take up to three years to master depending on the determination of the bird. The gwalygaloop also makes a distinctive call. To make this call they have to split their tongue. This is a very painful time for the gwalygaloop because their tongues are not split at birth. The continual call process eventually makes a slit. When their tongue is finally split, they make a frequent hic hic hicuuuuuuuuuuuuu. Once the male bird had found a mate, they stay together for life and produce up to 20 little gwalygaloopees.

Observation Hint:

Look in areas where they are few trees. Males have a red gobble hanging from their beaks. If they are hit by a car, they usually end up as a hood ornament. A good clue that some are in the area.

Ideas: _____ Organization: _____ Sentence Fluency: _____

Voice: _____ Word Choice: _____ Conventions: _____

Discussion of Student Work Examples

1. "All About Me"

Grade 5
Ideas: 2, 2
Organization: 2, 3
Sentence Fluency: 2–3, 3
Voice: 4, 4
Word Choice: 3, 3
Conventions: 4–5, 4

Comments: Halfway through, this piece seems to shift from "About the Author" to "What I Did Over Summer Vacation," adding irrelevant details and failing to elaborate on what could have been an interesting family account. Despite the catch of Sri Lanka, the author needs the spark of further details; he gets bogged down in generalities, such as "The next day, we went to Disneyland and thoroughly enjoyed ourselves." While the majority of the language is functional, a disproportionate number of sentences start with "I" (I've had . . . I have . . . I live . . . I have . . . I have . . . I come . . . etc.) The Voice, however, remains upbeat, consistent, and personal. Overall, it's a functional piece but without unexpected detail or interest.

2. "My Pet"

Grade 1
Ideas: 4, 4
Organization: 4, 5
Sentence Fluency: 3, 4
Voice: 3, 3
Word Choice: 3, 3
Conventions: 3, 4

Comments: One debate in trait-based assessment is whether expectations should be adjusted according to grade level or whether the traits should be seen as absolute, with more experienced students generally earning higher scores. This example was scored taking into account the student's young age. That said, this piece has some obvious problems, but also shows strong emergent writing. First, the author is generally aware of conventions—there are periods and capitals where needed, which define precise sentences. Obviously the student needs to continue to work on his/her spelling. Also, the organization is fairly smooth; the author offers an opening ("My pet is a fish.") and a conclusion ("I love Fliper."), with coherent thoughts in between. He/she also offers one rather unique idea: "I wonder what he sees." This student seems grade appropriate in his/her "mistakes" and could be encouraged to continue his/her path toward sentence fluency, voice, and use of more specific words.

3. "Gwalygaloop"

Grade 6
Ideas: 5, 5
Organization: 3, 4
Sentence Fluency: 3–4, 4
Voice: 4–5, 4–5
Word Choice: 4, 4
Conventions: 3–4, 3

Comments: Can you picture the gwalygaloop making an Ooooooo, Ahhhhhhh sound as it lays square eggs? This creative piece makes the reader smile with specific details and strong description. Words such as "membrane," "distinctive," "low plains area," and "red gobble" show the author's familiarity with wildlife descriptions and help the author pull off the assumed voice. You can tell the author enjoys this piece and so do we. However, though the piece generally follows the life cycle of the poor gwalygaloop, at times it sounds like an unrelated string of facts, detracting from the score for Organization. Sentence Fluency, while strong in each individual sentence, sounds a bit choppy when read as a whole; the author could vary his sentence structure to create more flow. Paragraphs also would increase a score in Organization.

Two Methods for Adjusting the Scoring Rubric

If using the Traits of Good Writing in your content area classes or with content-specific assignments, you may want to use one of the following two methods for transforming the basic rubric.

• Weighting the Traits

The relative importance of each trait is not the same for every assignment. For example, after reading a current events article, you may wish to check a student's written response for comprehension, thus choosing to place an emphasis on Ideas; likewise, for an illustrated poster, you may weigh Presentation higher than the other traits. Using a flexible rubric to weigh the traits has the advantage of accentuating the most important points of the assignment, while continuing to give at least token credit for writing style. Use the Weighted Scoring Rubric Template on page 85 to emphasize whichever traits are most important in any given assignment.

• Personalizing Assessment Criteria

In some assignments, the standard assessment criteria for the Traits of Good Writing don't speak specifically to what you want. For example, if the assignment were to create a comic strip showing the journey of food through the digestive system, you might score students based primarily on their demonstrated knowledge of the parts of the digestive system (esophagus, stomach, etc.). The standard method of scoring Ideas might not be quite enough. By "plugging in" a separate rubric to the Ideas slot, you could give students points for described piece of the digestive system. You may choose to keep the standard criteria for the rest of the traits, or you could plug in as many specifics as you like. This personalized system is the preferred method for integrating the Traits of Good Writing into content area classes.

Weighted Scoring Rubric Example (using standard assessment criteria)

Assignment: Paper describing the effects of acid rain

	5	3	1	Points	Weight	Total
Ideas	The paper's central idea is clear and focused and is supported by vivid, relevant details. All needed information is included.	The writer has defined a topic, but it is supported by few or by mundane details.	The writer has not defined a topic and details are lacking or irrelevant.	4	5	20
Word Choice	The writer uses precise, natural, and engaging words to convey the intended message.	While the writer's meaning is clear, word choice lacks energy; words are functional but routine.	Words are used incorrectly or the writer uses such limited vocabulary that meaning is impaired.	3.5	2	7
Voice	The writer is obviously aware of the audience, communicating in an engaging and personal tone.	While functional, the voice is impersonal; the piece could have been written by anybody.	The writer seems indifferent to his/her audience or topic; readers are unmoved and left flat.	3	1	3
Sentence Fluency	Sentences flow easily and are a pleasure to read aloud.	The text is mechanical rather than musical.	The text can be read aloud only with practice. Many structural problems exist.	3	2	6
Organization	Organization supports the topic and moves the reader through the text cleanly.	Readers find meaning without undue confusion, but their path is indirect.	There is no identifiable structure. Events and information are random.	3.5	1	3.5
Conventions	Even complex conventions enhance meaning and readability. Errors are few.	The writer has control of the basic conventions but struggles to use anything more complex.	Errors make the piece difficult to read. The writer uses basic conventions incorrectly.	2.5	2	5
Presentation	Layout and presentation enhance meaning and visual appeal.	The piece is readable and neat, neither adding to nor detracting from meaning and appeal.	Presentation is distracting or messy, making meaning unclear.	4	4	16
Total Points Possible (sum of "weight" column, times 5) 85						**Total Points Earned** 60.5

Weighted Scoring Rubric Template

				Points	Weight	Total
Ideas						
Word Choice						
Voice						
Sentence Fluency						
Organization						
Conventions						
Presentation						
Total Points Possible (sum of "weight" column, times 5)						**Total Points Earned**

Scoring Rubric Example (using some or all adjusted assessment criteria)

Assignment: Cartoon strip showing the path of food through the digestive tract

	Points: 30	Points: 15	Points: 0	Points Earned
Ideas	Demonstrates understanding of esophagus, stomach, duodenum, small intestine, large intestine, and rectum.	Understanding of the digestive tract is incomplete.	No demonstrated understanding of the digestive tract.	29
Word Choice	Points: 20	Points: 10	Points: 0	20
	Words from Ideas are used correctly.	Words from Ideas are used, but some are used improperly or are missing.	Content area vocabulary is lacking.	
Voice	Points: 10	Points: 5	Points: 0	9
	Includes humor, creativity, and zest in writing and drawing.	Solid product, but could have been created by anyone.	Completely bland and dry cartoons.	
Sentence Fluency	Points: 5	Points: 3	Points: 1	5
	Standard Criteria	Standard Criteria	Standard Criteria	
Organization	Points: 20	Points: 10	Points: 0	20
	Shows correct sequence of food through digestive tract.	Care is taken, but the path of food is slightly incorrect.	No demonstrated understanding of the sequence of food.	
Conventions	Points: 5	Points: 3	Points: 1	5
	Standard Criteria	Standard Criteria	Standard Criteria	
Presentation	Points: 10	Points: 5	Points: 10	10
	Five drawings are neatly done in colored pen with carefully handwritten annotations.	At least three drawings with some care are shown.	Drawings are missing, incomplete, or very sloppy.	

Total Points Possible	Total Points Earned
100	98

Scoring Rubric Template

	Points:	Points:	Points:	Points Earned
Ideas				
Word Choice	Points:	Points:	Points:	
Voice	Points:	Points:	Points:	
Sentence Fluency	Points:	Points:	Points:	
Organization	Points:	Points:	Points:	
Conventions	Points:	Points:	Points:	
Presentation	Points:	Points:	Points:	
	Total Points Possible		**Total Points Earned**	

Possible Scoring Pitfalls

While we would like to look at each student and each trait in its own bubble, it is sometimes difficult to separate scoring from context and from our own experience (Muschla, 2002). Be especially aware of the following, in the hopes of eliminating bias in your trait-based assessment:

• Trait Carryover

If a paper earns a low score on sentence fluency, for example, bias tends to pull other traits lower as well. As much as possible, try to rate each trait on its own merits, rather than allowing your scoring of other traits to cloud the picture. This can be especially difficult when trying to read content through a maze of jumbled conventions. Remember, just because a student can't spell *cat* does not mean that this student placed his/her attempt at the word in the wrong place organizationally.

• Presentation

A messy paper is not necessarily a poorly written paper. Although scribbles on a ripped page annoy teachers because of the lack of care, leave the low score where it belongs—in your assessment of presentation. Likewise, the word-processed copy inserted in a cover or bound with yarn may be hiding a lack of content. Be aware of prejudging content based on appearance.

• Length

Sometimes length is needed to describe a topic; at other times, students will create volume by decreasing density. A longer paper may or may not even be a fair representation of effort. If a student can sustain content over multiple pages, great! If not, you should encourage him/her to say more with less.

• Topic

In allowing students to write about authentic topics, you will undoubtedly read papers you don't like. Perhaps students will express political or social views with which you disagree. On the other hand, a student may pull at your heartstrings with a topic to which you relate or that evokes sympathy, such as difficult family circumstances. In both cases, try to score the writing independently of the topic. However, if a paper stirs emotions in you, perhaps the paper has, in fact, succeeded in doing so due to content.

• Inappropriate Content

Even in Authentic Writing, there are limits to what is acceptable in the classroom. Before giving students free reign, you will need to define your level of comfort with profanity, violence, intolerance, and writing that is designed to make others feel bad, and you will need to share your views with the class. Your school or district may have specific policies regarding inappropriate content. Depending on the severity, you may ask for revisions before assessing the work or, if school policy supports you, refuse to give credit for inappropriate work.

However, strong language or violent scenes are sometimes appropriate to describe events, and while you may not like the way something is said, vulgarity will likely not affect traits such as organization. You may need to separate your opinion from the grading scale. When in doubt, take refuge in the scoring guide and in the policies of your district.

• Low in the Stack

By the time you reach your 30th paper of the evening, the thought of a cup of tea and a soft pillow can make you rush through your remaining assignments. While you wrote detailed comments on the first ten, you may now find yourself spouting scores based on only the Introduction. Your students put a considerable amount of effort into their writing, and as painful as it can be at ten o'clock on a weeknight, they deserve a thorough read.

The key is in organizing your time such that you avoid late nights. Set aside a short time each day for assessment, and stick to it. Certainly there are ways to cut corners in assessment, but be careful to remain true to each paper. Also, when using the Writing Workshop, you may be able to create a steady trickle of finished work, rather than finding yourself inundated with papers turned in with a traditional due date.

• Hard Work

It may be difficult to give Thomas a "1" on Conventions after watching him pour every ounce of possible effort into an assignment. Again, do your best to remain impartial. When Thomas finally starts to improve, the higher scores will be earned as opposed to being hollow—a true achievement! Fortunately, there are ways we will look at later in this chapter when grading (as opposed to assessing) to take effort into account.

Common Difficulties with Trait-Based Assessment

As with any new skill, there will be a period of learning before you are proficient with Trait-Based Assessment and, like most activities, you will end up ironing out the majority of your difficulties through trial and error. However, just as you will ask your writing students to discover for themselves many of the techniques they will use and will also guide them to use established techniques, so too is it useful to see how others have solved some of the common difficulties associated with the traits. Specifically, we will look at the following two issues that commonly derail teachers' use of the traits:

- "My trait assessment doesn't fit the standard grading scale."

- "Trait assessment just takes too long!"

Problem: "My trait assessment doesn't fit the standard grading scale."

An average seven-trait assessment score is 3/5 for each trait. Thus, if assessing all seven traits, an average total score is 21/35. This translates to 60%, or a D on the standard grading scale! Obviously, you would rather not give your average students Ds. The numbers generated in trait-based assessment work well for the purpose of differentiating instruction, but when turning assessment into a grade, you will need to transform the numbers using one of two methods.

Solution 1: Use Writing Process Packet Materials to "Pad" Seven-Trait Assessment

As part of a writing workshop, you may ask students to turn in a packet of material demonstrating their use of each step in the writing process. Thus, in addition to the published copy of a student's work, you would have sheets for prewriting, drafting, revising, editing, etc. While you will assess the published copy using the Traits of Good Writing, you can give points for these additional packet materials when defining a grade:

Advantages

A. Rewards organization and study skills by forcing students to keep track of packet materials.

B. Reinforces writing process by giving points for evidence of the various writing steps, rather than for only the finished product.

Disadvantages

Requires a packet of material for each assignment, and thus works better for major projects.

Example:

In the assignment shown on the Packet Grading Cover Sheet on page 96, the trait score of 22/35 is padded by 60 points earned by additional packet materials, bringing the total score to 82/100. When grading the steps of the writing process using the Packet Grading Cover Sheet, scan for completion, inclusion, and effort rather than taking the time to assess each piece thoroughly. You will give specific feedback through trait-based assessment of the published writing. For example, when assigning points for the cover page, you would give five points merely for it being stapled to the front of the packet; you would scan the prewrite for effort and a reasonable number of ideas; and students who included a draft, revisions, peer/adult critique, and proofreading would generally earn close to full points simply for being organized and responsible enough to staple all required sheets into a packet. If you choose slightly different writing process steps, consider modifying the included Packet Grading Cover Sheet Template on page 97 to meet your needs.

Solution 2: Adjust Seven-Trait Assessment to Fit the Standard Grading Scale

The following method can be understood either by working through the theory or simply by applying the formula and noticing the appropriate scores it generates. If you choose not to collect assignment packets or to use the seven-trait assessment in grading smaller assignments for which you do not require a full packet of materials, you may adjust seven-trait assessment scores using the following formula:

Overall Score = 50 (Sum of points earned/sum of points possible) + 45

With this formula, you first create a percentage out of your seven-trait assessment score and weigh it out of 50 points. You then pad the score with an additional 45 points. This method also works well when choosing not to assess all seven traits. The formula generates the following scores from trait-based assessment. As you can see, these scores convert directly to the standard percentages for grades A to F.

Seven-Trait Score (per trait)	Converted Percent
1/5	55%
2/5	65%
3/5	75%
4/5	85%
5/5	95%

Advantages

A. Creates a median of C.

B. Works well for assignments without supporting materials in the form of assignment packets.

Disadvantages

With 5/5 = 95% (as shown in the table above), a perfect score still misses five points. If you like, you can create a criteria through which students can earn these extra five points, such as Author's Chair performance or an extra-credit activity sheet.

Example:

We graded Marisa's assignment on only five of the seven traits of good writing. She got 19/25, so:

Overall Score = 50 (Sum of points earned/sum of points possible) + 45
Overall Score = 50 (19/25) + 45 = 83

So Marisa got a B. Without using the equation adjustment, she would have gotten 19/25 = 0.76, or a C—not fair considering that she got mostly 4/5 scores on each trait assessed.

Problem: "Trait assessment just takes too long!"

It's true that trait-based assessment will likely be cumbersome at first, but once you are able to call to mind the specifics of each trait without referencing the rubric, your speed will increase dramatically. Also, keep in mind the following when looking to increase your per-paper time:

- Although you will be assigning a score, the actual number is far less important than finding the trait(s) on which each student needs work. Again, focus on assessing, rather than grading—if five of Thomas' traits show a significantly higher level of mastery than do the other two, there is no reason to agonize over whether these two lagging traits should be scored a 1 or a 2. You have found the areas in which he needs to work; target them with differentiated lessons.

- There is no need to assess every trait on every assignment. If you teach a lesson about prewriting and ask students to complete an assignment based on the lesson, you may score each paper simply for organization. If you reinforce a grammar lesson with a short assignment, you may score the assignment solely on conventions. If you decide to collect assignments after the drafting stage, students haven't yet edited their work and you could choose to exclude conventions from the seven-trait assessment. Consider which traits are applicable to each assignment and assess accordingly.

- Use the traits to comment on student writing rather than taking the time to write lengthy descriptive comments on each paper.

- Target only certain students for more in-depth assessment. Some students may need more direction than others.

- Choose one (or perhaps two) traits to assess while students read their work aloud during Author's Chair. Without looking at the published copy, you will still be able to assign an accurate score to Ideas, Word Choice, Sentence Fluency and, potentially, Voice and Organization.

- Instruct students to give oral feedback using the language of the traits. While not necessarily a thorough assessment, conferencing in peer groups and during the revision process allows significant feedback without an unnecessary draw on your time.

Packet Grading Cover Sheet Example

Cover Page (5)			5
Prewrite (10)			7
Draft (10)			10
Revision (10)			10
Peer/Adult Critique (5)			5
Incorporating Comments (10)			10
Proofreading (10)			8
Peer/Adult Edit (5)			5
Published Work (35)	Ideas	3	
	Organization	4	
	Voice	3	
	Sentence Fluency	3	} 22
	Word Choice	3	
	Conventions	2	
	Presentation	4	
		Total Score:	82

Excerpted from *Implementing an Effective Writing Program* by Kristi Pikiewicz and Garth Sundem. Copyright ©2004 by Shell Education.

Packet Grading Cover Sheet Template

Name: _____ Date: _____ Assignment: _____

Cover Page (5)		
Prewrite (10)		
Draft (10)		
Revision (10)		
Peer/Adult Critique (5)		
Incorporating Comments (10)		
Proofreading (10)		
Peer/Adult Edit (5)		
Published Work (35)	Ideas (5)	
	Organization (5)	
	Voice (5)	
	Sentence Fluency (5)	
	Word Choice (5)	
	Conventions (5)	
	Presentation (5)	
	Total Score:	

Chapter 4 Reflection

1. If you plan to use the Traits of Good Writing in your classroom, describe when and how you will do so.

   _____

   _____

   _____

   _____

2. In your opinion, what are some advantages of the Traits of Good Writing when compared to rubric, holistic, or portfolio assessment?

   _____

   _____

   _____

   _____

3. How can you use the Traits of Good Writing to assess content area assignments?

   _____

   _____

   _____

   _____

Teaching Using the Traits of Good Writing

The first step in implementing the Traits of Good Writing in your classroom (after you have explored them yourself) is to teach these traits to your students. If, for example, you simply return assignments with a list of traits and 1–5 scores, your students will have little idea how these numbers relate to their writing and will miss out on important opportunities to interact with writing using these traits. In order to use the traits in peer revision while drafting their own writing, in discussing examples, to comprehend your lessons, and while revising their own work, students will need to have a clear picture of what exactly each of these traits represents and also what the traits look like in real writing (Spandel, 2004).

Introductory Trait Lessons

Pages 101–108 include examples of short lessons to help students learn the Traits of Good Writing. In each, the trait to be taught is conspicuously lacking in the example. After using the included description to discuss the trait, you will instruct your class to collaborate to revise the excerpt with the trait in mind. You could either have them first work independently or do it as a whole-class exercise. As they get stuck, prompt them using the suggestions on pages 109–112. After revising each example, your students could write a short description of the trait in their writing notebooks. After teaching a trait, make sure to use trait vocabulary whenever possible to reinforce its use.

In addition to these lessons, you can reinforce the traits by finding your own examples and revising them with the help of your class. By drawing your revision excerpts from published materials, you will also help students see the Traits of Good Writing as a real-world tool, as opposed to an exercise applicable only to the classroom. The following are good sources of revision materials:

- Picture books (especially for Voice, Word Choice, and Presentation) (Culham, 2004)

- Newspapers (especially for Organization, Sentence Fluency, and Ideas)

- Websites (especially for Conventions and Presentation)

- Historic primary source documents, such as Civil War letters from *http://www.memory.loc.gov/ ammem* (good for all traits)

- Textbooks (especially for Presentation, Organization, and Ideas)

- Literature (especially for Sentence Fluency, Word Choice, and Voice)

Ideas

Ideas are the information in your writing. What happens in your story, or what do you want the reader to know? In a good piece of writing, there is one main idea (topic) and many little ideas (details) that support the topic. Good details are things the reader doesn't already know or doesn't expect—the more specific and interesting an idea, the better. For example, a not-so-good idea in a story about a dog might be "the dog had four legs"—we already expect this! An interesting idea might be that the dog "loved little kids but growled at strollers."

Directions: Add ideas to the following story.

John got out of bed and got ready for school. He went to school. John had fun during recess. He ate the school lunch. After school, John played sports. Then, he went to sleep.

_____

_____

_____

_____

_____

_____

_____

_____

_____

Word Choice

The best word choice is the most specific word choice. For example, instead of saying that someone "went" to the store, we could say they "ran." Actually, instead of just saying "ran," we could say they "sprinted," "jogged," or "loped." Good word choice tells exactly how something happened or what something is. Word choice helps the reader paint a picture in his/her mind. For example, if a stove is "hot," is it "scalding," "sizzling," "blistering," or just "warm"?

Directions: Revise the following passage for word choice. Change words to make them more specific.

When John woke up this morning, he felt good. He heard chickadees squawking and opened his curtains to the light of the big sun. The weather was nice and made him feel like something good. He got up and went downstairs, where his big brother was already eating cereal.

"Good morning, Brother," John's big brother said.

"Good morning, Brother," John said. John put two things of sugar on his cereal and smiled, thinking about what was going to be a good day.

_____

_____

_____

_____

_____

_____

_____

_____

_____

Sentence Fluency

Good sentence fluency makes writing that is easy to read aloud. You don't have to stop and start and you don't get jumbled up, even the first time you try to read something. Also, not all sentences sound the same—in a piece with good sentence fluency, the writer uses many different lengths and avoids always starting a sentence with the same word. Sometimes weird sentence fluency can come from words being out of place.

Directions: Revise the following passage for sentence fluency by changing some of the first words and sentence lengths.

I love school lunch. It's always totally yummy. I like hamburgers best. I don't like mustard. I don't use mustard. I always finish first. I even eat the coleslaw.

_____

_____

_____

_____

_____

_____

_____

_____

_____

_____

_____

Voice

Voice creates the personality of a piece of writing. Is it "businesslike," "fun," "silly," "educated," or "excited"? One voice may not be right for all audiences—if you were writing a story for a kindergartner, it would have a different voice than if you were writing a research paper for your teacher. In a piece with a strong voice, you can hear the author's excitement about and interest in the topic, and you can tell who wrote it.

Directions: The example below is written for a group of business people—revise it so that its voice is appropriate for a children's story.

The cow in question, named Betsy, spent the vast majority of the day consuming roughage and then chewing said roughage while standing and considering her life choices. While she was quite enamored of roughage, she felt her life was lacking a certain element of interest. Said cow decided after much deliberation to take over the world.

_____

_____

_____

_____

_____

_____

_____

_____

_____

_____

_____

Organization

For a piece to have good organization, everything needs to be in the right place and the writing needs to have some sort of bigger structure. Organization in writing is like driving from one place to another without taking all sorts of detours. Also, all the little ideas in a piece fit in paragraphs under the bigger ideas. For example, a paragraph about skydiving might have information about parachutes, being scared, and what the ground looks like from way up high, but it probably wouldn't have a description of leaf-cutting ants.

Directions: Help! The underlined sentences below are out of place—revise this example to give the piece better organization. You may have to delete some sentences that don't fit anywhere.

Skateboarding is an activity many students enjoy and, despite the fact that some think it can be dangerous, should be allowed on the school playground. <u>Especially some of the students who are the best skateboarders feel like school administrators don't care what they think</u>. Allowing skateboards on the playground would make students happier about their school, would give students something to do other than the standard playground sports, and could be done in a way that is both safe for kids and legally safe for the school. <u>Second, parents would have to sign a permission slip that would keep them from suing the school if their child got hurt</u>.

Sometimes students think that school is just a place where they have to follow all sorts of dumb rules, and they can never have any fun. <u>While some people like basketball, four-square, and tag, others don't</u>. Allowing skateboarding on the playground would help these students see that administrators care about them, and that administrators want school to be a fun place as well as a place to learn. <u>Tightrope walking is another activity that would be a fun recess activity</u>.

Allowing skateboards on the playground would give students another option for recess recreation, thus helping some students who might otherwise just stand around and talk stay active. Playgrounds should be for everybody, not just the people who enjoy team sports.

By following a couple of simple rules, we could make skateboarding on the playground safe both for kids and for the school. <u>Finally, there would have to be a designated area for skateboarding only so that kids who weren't on boards didn't get run over</u>. First, kids would have to wear helmets, wrist guards, and knee pads whenever they ride.

Organization *(cont.)*

As you can see, there are many reasons why skateboards should be allowed on the playground, and there's a way we can all do it safely. <u>A BMX track would also be nice</u>. I hope you will reevaluate school rules and let kids skateboard on the playground.

_____

_____

_____

_____

_____

_____

_____

_____

_____

_____

_____

_____

_____

_____

_____

_____

_____

Conventions

Conventions make writing *right*. Anytime the teacher picks up the red pen, there's probably a problem with conventions. Spelling, grammar, punctuation, capitalization, and paragraphing are all things that have to do with conventions.

Directions: The following paragraph has many errors in conventions. See if you can find them all. Use a red pen to mark and correct all the errors.

On January 31st and Feb 1st, teams of the top junoir cross-country ski rasers from across the intermountain region will compete at lindley park. This, the second of three Junyer Olympic qualifiers, will bring teams from idaho, utah, and montana to compete against Bozeman's own Bridger Ski Foundation youths, including hopeful Nathan Park, who will try to live up to the high standards set by last year's national juniors champions leif zimmerman and Kristina Trygstaad-Saari. races start at 10 A.M. Saturday with sprints divided into age groups. For easy access, park in the hosbittal lots off Highland Blvd. Bring your puffy coat and your cowbells.

Sunday features longer races. Believe it or not, a beyootifel 15K is groomed into Lindley Park. On either day, regular folks of any age can pit their thighs against the youths in sprint, 10K (female), or 15K (male) format. Registration is $18 per race. look for details on the B.S.F. website (**http://www.xcbozeman.org**) or ask at Bangtail bike and Ski on main St.

Presentation

When you present your finished work, it should be neat, clean, and legible. Also, if you created a project such as a poster or picture book, your presentation should make your words easier (not harder!) to understand. Presentation draws readers in and makes them want to take a second look.

Directions: Working as individuals, organize the information below on a page, as if you were making a poster. Add any illustrations you think it needs, and don't forget that some of these words should be titles.

Science Fair Project

"Do beans grow better inside or outside?"

I planted one group of beans outside where they would get light from the sun and another set inside where they would get light through a window and from electric lights. I tried to keep everything else the same and was lucky that the temperature outside was close to the temperature inside. I found that beans grow better outside.

Revision Directions for Introductory Trait Lessons

Ideas

Ideas could be added to the story by answering any of the following questions about John:

- What woke John up, and how did he feel about getting out of bed?

- What did John do to get ready for school that most people wouldn't think of?

- How did John get to school? What difficulties did he have along the way?

- What did John do during recess that was so much fun?

- What did John eat for school lunch? What was it like? Describe it using all five senses.

- How did John feel when the school day ended?

- Describe in detail what he did after school—what interesting things happened?

- How did John feel as he went to sleep?

- Could anything that happened to John earlier have affected what happened to him later?

Word Choice

The following is a possible revision, with changed words underlined:

When John woke up this morning, he felt <u>like a million bucks</u>. He heard chickadees <u>chirping</u> and <u>threw open</u> his curtains to the light of the <u>smiling</u> sun. The weather was <u>delightful</u> and made him feel like <u>lying on his back in the middle of a field of tall grass</u>. He <u>sprang out of bed</u> and <u>almost tumbled</u>

downstairs, where his big brother was already <u>scarfing Cheerios</u>.

"<u>Yo, bro. What's up</u>?" John's big brother <u>mumbled</u>.

"<u>*I'm up*</u>!" John <u>crowed</u>. John <u>heaped</u> two <u>gargantuan teaspoons</u> of <u>moist brown sugar</u> on his <u>Cornflakes</u> and <u>grinned</u>, <u>pondering</u> what was sure to be a <u>splendid</u> day.

Sentence Fluency

Help students notice the repetitious, short sentence length and the repetition of the first word, *I*. To revise, show students how they can vary the sentence structure by combining two or more sentences using commas. Make sure your revision also deals with the issues of first word and sentence length.

Voice

Lead students in revising the example to come up with a version similar to the following:

Once upon a time there was a cow named Betsy. Betsy stood around all day eating grass and thinking about nothing in particular. She liked eating grass but couldn't help thinking there was something missing in her life. So Betsy decided to take over the world.

Organization

After revising, the class should come up with a paper similar to the following:

Skateboarding is an activity many students enjoy and, despite the fact that some think it can be dangerous, should be allowed on the school playground. Allowing skateboards on the playground would make students happier about their school, would give students something to do other than the standard playground sports, and could be done in a way that is both safe for kids and legally safe for the school.

Sometimes students think that school is just a place where they have to follow all sorts of rules, and that they can never have any fun. Some of the students who are the best skateboarders feel that school administrators don't care what they think. Allowing skateboarding on the playground would help these students see that administrators care about them, and that administrators want school to be a fun place as well as a place to learn.

While some people like basketball, four-square, and tag, others don't. Allowing skateboards on the playground would give students another option for recess recreation, thus helping some students, who might otherwise just stand around and talk, stay active. Playgrounds should be for everybody, not just the people who enjoy team sports.

By following a couple of simple rules, we could make skateboarding on the playground safe both for kids and for the school. First, kids would have to wear helmets, wrist guards, and knee pads whenever they ride. Also, parents would have to sign a permission slip that would keep them from suing the school if their child got hurt. Finally, there would have to be a designated area for skateboarding only, so that kids who aren't on boards don't get run over.

As you can see, there are many reasons why skateboards should be allowed on the playground, and there's a way we can all do it safely. I hope you will reevaluate school rules and let kids skateboard on the playground.

Conventions

Students should find and correct all mistakes (corrected paragraph shown below).

> On January 31st and February 1st, teams of the top junior cross-country ski racers from across the intermountain region will compete at Lindley Park. This, the second of three Junior Olympic qualifiers, will bring teams from Idaho, Utah, and Montana to compete against Bozeman's own Bridger Ski Foundation youths, including hopeful Nathan Park, who will try to live up to the high standards set by last year's national juniors champions Leif Zimmerman and Kristina Trygstaad-Saari. Races start at 10 A.M. Saturday, with sprints divided into age groups. For easy access, park in the hospital lots off Highland Blvd. Bring your puffy coat and your cowbells.
>
> Sunday features longer races. Believe it or not, a beautiful 15K is groomed into Lindley Park. On either day, regular folks of any age can pit their thighs against the youths in sprint, 10K (female), or 15K (male) format. Registration is $18 per race. Look for details on the B.S.F. website (*http://www.xcbozeman.org*) or ask at Bangtail Bike and Ski on Main St.

Presentation

Give students time to organize and illustrate the information included in the example. Ask volunteers to show their work and discuss the presentation with a focus on how students used presentation to highlight meaning. Include a discussion on what aspects of legibility and cleanliness could be improved (i.e., was it written on lined, on ripped paper, in pencil, in pen?.).

The Traits of Good Writing in Instruction

While the basis of the Traits of Good Writing is an assessment rubric, you may also use the traits while instructing.

Differentiation Using the Trait Assessment Data

Once you have assessed, you can use the scores to choose lessons that are relevant to each student (Betts, 2004). You might ask the student who had the lowest-scoring trait to take special care with this trait on the next project or provide the student with extra practice on the trait. You can also use the traits to differentiate on a per-class basis. For example, you may notice that your class's use of word choice lags behind other scores. In this case, you may choose to target the class with a lesson on word choice.

The same is true of choosing small groups. No longer do we designate "bluebirds," "redbirds," and "finches" for groups based on reading level (Caldwell & Ford, 2002). Today's small group is flexible, convened perhaps just for a few minutes in the course of one class period. In the next class period, you might create different groups altogether. Using the traits, if you notice that, for example, three students struggle with their use of ideas, you might pull them aside for a little extra help while other students are working independently.

However, differentiating isn't always easy. Like yesteryear's one-room schoolhouse, we have many different instructional levels in our classrooms, and we need to find ways to teach each of these levels within our existing frameworks (Tomlinson, 2004). The crux of differentiating instruction (other than assessing in order to learn where each student needs additional work) is in finding time to do it. If there were eight teachers in the classroom, it would be easy—each would work with a small group of students with similar needs, and these groups would change daily. However, there's only one of you, and your time is precious.

In the Writing Workshop, if you can manage independent work such that it is truly independent, you will have time to work with students in either small group or individual settings. The key to this strategy is efficiency. Make sure students know what is expected of them during independent work time, as well as during small group instruction. You may only have ten to 15 minutes to work with a small group, so make sure that each student knows what he/she will need for the lesson, and that he/she is able to transition to the area of your classroom set aside for small group instruction with little downtime. When planning small group instruction, take a minute at the end of your mini lesson to let your class know who should move to the small group instruction area and what they should bring with them. This allows only one unsettled time while the class moves into independent work and your small group gets ready for further instruction.

In addition to differentiating your instruction based on which students are performing below expectation on certain traits, also consider teaching small group lessons for the students who are excelling in a trait. In addition, you may consider mixing struggling students into high-level small group instruction, such that your higher students benefit from a chance to extend their skills while your struggling students have a chance to learn from their more advanced peers.

Differentiating on an individual basis is a bit more difficult, as you simply don't have the time to work individually with every student every day. One solution is to use targeted lessons that students will be able to complete independently. For example, instead of trying to work one-on-one with a student, you might hand him/her directions for short, additional practice and move on. Of course, activity sheets or their like are no substitute for personal help, but when your time is tight, there may not be another good option. Be careful in your use of lessons guided by activity sheets; instead, consider using them as another tool in your teaching kit.

Using the Language of the Traits

The traits provide the vocabulary you and your students can use to evaluate any writing (Hoover, 2001). By noticing how authors use the traits, students will gain a clearer idea of how to apply the traits in their own writing. Strive to integrate the traits into any conversation or discussion, creating no distinction between times that you are in "trait mode" and times that you are simply teaching writing—the traits *are* writing! Encourage students to use trait vocabulary in small groups, peer revision, and while giving comments following an Author's Chair. In fact, the more integrated the traits are in your instruction, the more students will learn to recognize and manipulate them in their own writing.

Trait-Based Lessons

Trait-based lessons make a clear use of mini lessons, if you are formatting your class as a writing workshop. For example, you might start a class period with a lesson on how to revise for word choice. Another day, you could combine traits, focusing on how ideas are organized into paragraphs. Potentially, you could start every class period with a quick trait-based lesson before asking students to continue their Authentic Writing assignments during independent work. If you are focusing more on direct instruction, you can easily design lessons that teach, practice, and then assess students' use of one or more of the traits. Remember to differentiate your instruction based on class needs.

When designing mini lessons, be aware of the following things:

- Teach one skill only, with high takeaway value.

- You need not pair every lesson with an assessment; if you do, consider discussing to gauge retention.

- Try to create routine with your mini lessons in format and usage.

- Don't worry about teaching lessons you find a bit boring—a mini lesson is short enough that even if it's "nuts-and-bolts" material, students will be able to remain involved.

- Make sure to reference your district standards so that your mini lessons support specific curriculum elements.

- Consider collaborating with a team of teachers at your school to organize lessons for use with every trait. Some districts are now sponsoring summer workshops in which teachers write district-specific lessons based on the traits.

- For a ready-to-use compilation of lessons matched to every trait and every score in a full class, small group, and individual format (stand-alone and revision), reference *Implementing an Effective Writing Program* (Pikiewicz & Sundem, 2004).

Monitoring Progress Through the Traits of Good Writing

As instructors, teaching is a means to an end. Our goal is not to teach but to help students learn. Despite differentiating instruction based on trait assessment, if we don't ensure progress, we haven't achieved our goal.

One of the dangers in using the Traits of Good Writing is in the potential for each student to receive a hodge-podge of lessons, without a focused goal. On one assignment, a student may show the need for help with Organization, which you give as part of a small group lesson. On the next assignment, it looks like the student could use significant work on Word Choice, which you find time to offer individually. In large group lessons, you insert grammar and writing process strategies. Certainly, the student is consistently receiving quality instruction, but how can you ensure that the instruction is affecting the student's skills? A simple solution is to monitor the evolution of trait-based assessment scores throughout the year (Hoover, 2001).

The Seven-Trait Progress Chart on page 120 can also help you stay organized. Keep the Seven-Trait Progress Chart on hand while assessing students' completed work. Note their scores on the progress chart and refer to it as a master list. If administrators, parents, or support staff have questions as to a student's relative level or growth as a writer, you can easily refer them to the progress chart.

In addition, you can use the chart to demonstrate classroom levels as a whole. The Seven-Trait Progress Chart provides a visual representation of your entire class, and as such is a good tool to use when planning mini lessons and small group lessons. Pinpoint your students' difficulties and teach mini lessons on these topics.

Also, by noticing students' scores across a number of assignments, you will get a clear picture of which traits each student consistently scores high and low on. Perhaps you will choose to target Ideas rather than Conventions with a lesson based on a student's score history, even though the scores for these two traits on the most recent assignment are the same.

However, the chart brings with it the possibility of influencing assessment scores. Despite our best efforts, students will not always progress. Learning how to write is a process that frequently happens with two steps forward, offset by one step back. In general, students will learn, but we shouldn't expect every seven-trait score to be higher than it was on the previous assignment. If, for example, Anna earned straight 4s on the last assignment, don't let the scores influence you into awarding 4s or 5s for the next assignment, which may or may not be deserved. To combat the tendency to score higher with every assignment, assess a paper fully before marking the scores on the progress chart or cover past scores while you mark the new ones. While you will likely remember which students usually score high and low, you can remain as unbiased as possible by staying blind to past scores.

Remember, the Seven-Trait Progress Chart is as close to a numerical snapshot of your class as possible. Refer to it whenever you need data for lesson planning, small group composition, individual lessons, etc. Use the progress chart to easily implement assessment-driven instruction.

Seven-Trait Progress Chart Example

Class: _____ Period: _____ Dates: _____

	Assignments	About the Author	Hero Paper	Justifying Strange Pet	Expository Current Event	Scary Story	Design a Holiday	Debate a School Issue	Historical Narrative	Detail Description	Newspaper Article		
Names:	Ideas	2	3	2	2	3	3	2	3	3	4		
Emily Grayheart	Organization	4	4	3	4	3	4	4	4	3	4		
	Word Choice	3	3	4	3	4	3	4	5	4	5		
	Sent. Fluency	2	2	2	3	2	2	3	3	3	3		
	Voice	2	2	3	2	4	3	3	3	4	4		
	Conventions	1	1	2	1	2	2	3	2	3	3		
	Presentation	3	3	4	3	3	4	4	3	3	4		
Sean Hannity	Ideas	1	1	2	1	2	2	1	2	2	2		
	Organization	2	2	3	3	2	3	2	3	3	3		
	Word Choice	2	1	2	2	2	3	3	3	4	3		
	Sent. Fluency	1	2	1	1	2	2	2	1	2	3		
	Voice	1	1	1	2	2	1	2	2	2	2		
	Conventions	1	2	2	2	3	2	2	3	3	3		
	Presentation	3	3	2	3	3	4	3	4	3	4		
Peter Ramirez	Ideas	4	4	4	5	4	4	4	5	5	5		
	Organization	3	3	4	4	3	4	4	4	5	5		
	Word Choice	4	4	3	4	4	5	4	4	5	5		
	Sent. Fluency	3	4	3	4	4	3	3	4	4	4		
	Voice	3	2	3	3	2	3	3	4	3	4		
	Conventions	5	5	5	5	5	4	4	5	5	5		
	Presentation	2	2	2	2	3	3	3	2	3	4		

Excerpted from *Implementing an Effective Writing Program* by Kristi Pikiewicz and Garth Sundem. Copyright ©2004 by Shell Education.

Seven-Trait Progress Chart

Class: _____ Period: _____ Dates: _____

	Assignments											
Names:	Ideas											
	Organization											
	Word Choice											
	Sent. Fluency											
	Voice											
	Conventions											
	Presentation											
	Ideas											
	Organization											
	Word Choice											
	Sent. Fluency											
	Voice											
	Conventions											
	Presentation											
	Ideas											
	Organization											
	Word Choice											
	Sent. Fluency											
	Voice											
	Conventions											
	Presentation											

Chapter 5 Reflection

1. If you plan to use the Traits of Good Writing, when will you find time to help students understand the traits?

   _____

   _____

   _____

   _____

   _____

2. What does *differentiation* mean to you, and how will you use the Traits of Good Writing to achieve it?

   _____

   _____

   _____

   _____

   _____

3. What role will the Traits of Good Writing play in your day-to-day instruction?

   _____

   _____

   _____

   _____

   _____

Assignments

In combination with the writing process, Authentic Writing, and possibly a writing workshop, assignments can range the spectrum of guidance, from simply a due date for a student-chosen topic to a suggested length to a type of writing to an idea starter to an assigned topic to a series of short-answer questions. Outside the writing process, you may assign work to reinforce lessons or to help students with their understanding of the Traits of Good Writing.

Also, you may choose to spend class time completing assignments, or you might ask students to do the majority of their writing at home, leaving you more time for instruction (Hodapp & Hodapp, 1992). No matter which assignment strategy you use, by defining your ideas before diving in, you can create a logical flow and progression, rather than ending up with lots of assignments with little connection.

As discussed earlier, you will need to scaffold your students into Authentic Writing. Beginning on page 124 are assignment ideas for each of the four types of writing that you can use to move from directed topics to student-chosen work. Also included are shorter writing prompts for use in daily assignments or in journals.

Expository Prompts

Specific Topics

- Write a news story about a recent sports event you saw or participated in.
- Write a "how-to" guide for making new friends.
- Introduce your school to a new student.
- Describe the steps that someone has to take in order to get along with brothers or sisters.
- Research and write about the history of your school or home.

Guided Topics

- Write a news story about something volunteers have done in your community.
- Either create a new game and write the rules for it or write the rules for a game that you already know.
- Write about one problem you notice in the school cafeteria.
- Write to a local politician about something that needs to be changed in your community.
- Write a book or movie review.

Idea Starters

- Write a "how-to" article.
- Describe the history of an event.
- Write about a problem that you see in the world, *without* taking sides.
- Write a research report.
- Report on breaking news in your school or community.

Persuasive Prompts

Specific Topics

- Is television good or bad? Why?
- Should song lyrics be rated like movies?
- Why should weekends be longer?
- Why should or shouldn't a man be a stay-at-home dad while his wife works?
- What is more important—looks or personality? Why?
- Convince your parents that you deserve a larger allowance.
- Should animals be used for medical research?
- Should sex and violence on television or in the movies be restricted?
- Should Spanish-language instruction be available in U.S. public schools?
- Should schools have the right to require uniforms? Should students wear uniforms at school?

Guided Topics

- This school really needs . . .
- Convince the school administration that a school rule is unfair.
- Write a letter to the editor of your local paper, convincing readers to think a certain way about an issue in your community.
- Convince an employer that you are qualified for a job.
- Convince your parents to let you out of a household chore.

Idea Starters

- Convince your parents of something.
- Convince your teacher of something.
- Take a stand on a social/political issue.
- Convince a politician of something.
- Write about the *best* way to do something.

Descriptive Prompts

Specific Topics

- Take your class on an art walk—ask them to choose a painting to describe in words.
- Describe pizza to someone who has never tasted it.
- You're walking along and you see a scary house (or a vicious dog)—describe it to someone.
- Describe a house of the future.
- Describe the craziest outfit you can think of and the type of person that would wear it.

Guided Topics

- Describe something interesting that you have seen outdoors.
- Describe a cool store.
- What invention would you like to see in your lifetime?
- Describe the most beautiful thing you have ever seen.
- Describe a type of food.

Idea Starters

- Describe something you see every day.
- Describe something that is not real.
- Describe a scene from nature.
- Describe an event.
- Describe a person.

Narrative Prompts

Specific Topics

- Write about a day in the life of your pet.
- Write a story of you getting ready for school on a crazy morning.
- Write a story about learning how to ride a bicycle (or how to swim).
- Write about the first day of school this year.
- Write about the one favorite thing you did over summer vacation.

Guided Topics

- Retell your favorite family story.
- Write about a narrow escape from trouble or danger.
- Describe your craziest experience in a restaurant.
- Retell a fairy tale from a different point of view.
- Write a story that takes place in the school cafeteria.

Idea Starters

- Brainstorm characters, settings, and conflicts—mix and match them to create stories.
- Write an adventure or fantasy.
- Write a story that actually happened.
- Write a funny story.
- Write a sad story.

Daily Journal Prompts

Use these daily prompts as idea starters for students' writing journals, as guided writing for students who finish an assignment early, or as short take-home questions. Keep track of which prompts you have used by checking them off.

	Is television good?	I wish I didn't have to . . .
	How do you feel about your appearance?	What do you do for exercise?
	My idea of a fun weekend . . .	What parts of nature do you like best?
	What would you do if someone told you a joke that you didn't think was funny?	What do you think someone your age can do to help reduce the amount of pollution in our environment?
	What four things are most important in your life?	What would you invent to make life better?
	What are some examples of prejudice?	What do you think the world will be like when you are a grown-up?
	If you could do whatever you wanted to right now, what would you do?	What would you do if you wanted to be friends with someone who spoke no English?
	What would you do if your friend had a broken leg? How would you cheer him/her up?	What would you do if you were in the middle of the lake and your boat began to leak?
	What if cows gave root beer instead of milk?	What is something that makes you feel sad?
	What would happen if you found gold in your backyard?	What would happen if children ruled the world?
	What would happen if there were no cars, buses, trains, boats, or planes? How would this change your life?	What would you do if you woke up in another country and no one could understand you?
	What would happen if you threw a piece of trash on the ground? What if everyone did?	What would happen if you could fly whenever you wanted? When would you use this ability?
	What if all the streets were rivers? What would be different?	What is the worst thing parents can do to their children?
	Sometimes, adults seem . . .	What is a good neighbor?
	A dedicated teacher or coach I know . . .	What is something you dislike about yourself?
	My first encounter with a bully . . .	I couldn't believe that my mother volunteered me for that job!

Daily Journal Prompts *(cont.)*

What do you worry about?	Why are soap operas so popular?
What things do you think are beautiful?	A visit to a relative's house.
Rights that kids in my grade should have are . . .	What I've broken or lost that belongs to someone else.
We all make mistakes.	What can animals teach humans?
A meaningful gift I've given or received.	What would happen if you grew taller than trees? How would this change your life?
What's under my bed?	Something I don't understand.
Sometimes I wish . . .	The most fun I've had recently is . . .
An unforgettable dream.	I'm happy when . . .
I wonder why . . .	I've done something no one else has done.
My worst vacation.	Things that could be better in my neighborhood.
The hardest thing I've ever done is . . .	If I could be someone else, I would be . . .
What I know about the ocean.	Good things about my neighborhood.
A typical lunch hour includes . . .	A song that means a lot to me is . . .
I don't understand why . . .	If I suddenly had to move . . .
What is important to you?	My most embarrassing moment is . . .
Things I'd like to change about myself.	What if you were the teacher?
Book characters I'd like to meet are . . .	A place I'd like to visit is . . .
If I were principal for the day . . .	My first school memories are of . . .
What would you do if you found a magic wand?	One thing I want to do by the time I finish eighth grade is . . .

Glossary

assessment—the process of evaluating student work for the purpose of determining skills (as opposed to grading)

assignment packet—a packet of materials showing each step in the writing process

Authentic Spelling—a program that asks students to improve the spelling of words used in their own writing

Authentic Writing—writing in which students choose their own topic and publish their writing in a way that has real-world purpose

Author's Chair—a technique in the writing workshop where students read their finished work aloud

balanced literacy—a literacy program that includes the writing workshop, writing process, writing traits, and elements such as interactive and shared writing

best practices—the best teaching practices to the extent of current knowledge

bias in grading—factors other than what is written that influence grading or assessment

conventions—the mechanics of writing (spelling, grammar, etc.)

descriptive writing—writing that is devoid of plot; it simply describes

differentiation—teaching at different levels and with differing learning styles to meet the needs of diverse learners

direct instruction—lecture-format teaching

discovery-based learning—learning in which students discover information through their own explorations (rather than learning by listening or reading alone)

draft—the step in the writing process during which authors write their ideas in sentences and paragraphs

editing—the step in the writing process that focuses on revising for Conventions (as opposed to revision)

expository writing—nonfiction writing that describes information (reports, articles, letters)

flexible grouping—changing the composition of your small groups such that students are not tracked by ability

grading—assigning numbers to assignments simply for use in your grade book (as opposed to assessment)

holistic assessment—assessment based on the work as a whole

ideas—the writing trait that includes a topic and supporting details; good ideas are specific and unexpected

mini lesson—in the writing workshop, the short time at the beginning of class used for direct instruction

narrative writing—the type of writing that includes fiction or nonfiction stories

organization—the writing trait that focuses on how ideas are placed (ideas are relevant to their paragraph, there is an introduction and a conclusion, etc.)

peer revision—an optional step in the writing process and writing workshop in which students collaborate to revise each other's work

persuasive writing—the type of writing that is meant to convince the reader to think or act a certain way

presentation—the writing trait that focuses on the way the finished product looks; good presentation enhances the meaning of the text

prewrite—the step of the writing process in which authors brainstorm ideas and organize them in at least a rudimentary fashion

progress—proof that students are improving their writing skills

publish—the step of the writing process in which authors format their finished work for an audience

revision—the step of the writing process in which authors change elements of their draft with the intention of improving their work

rubric—a scoring guide for student work that defines how you will assess or assign points

scaffolding—working toward a difficult technique a little at a time; for example, you might scaffold students toward Authentic Writing by gradually releasing the constraints of your assignments

sentence fluency—the writing trait that focuses on readability and flow, both within individual sentences and across a piece of writing

Traits of Good Writing—a scoring rubric that independently assesses the components that make writing good (ideas, sentence fluency, voice, organization, word choice, conventions, presentation)

voice—the writing trait in which authors demonstrate their personality; voice should be appropriate to an assignment's audience and purpose and should demonstrate the author's passion for the topic

word choice—the writing trait that focuses on the individual words used; good word choice paints a specific mental image

writing process—the process that all authors use to prewrite, draft, revise, and publish their work

writing workshop—a framework for classroom time in which a mini lesson is followed by independent student work, ending with a brief time for sharing

References

Adams, P. (1991). Revising: An approach for all seasons. *Writing Notebook: Creative Word Processing in the Classroom, 9(2)*, 11–12.

Barlow, B. (2001). Journaling. *Instructor, 111(1)*, 44.

Bartch, J. (1992). An alternative to spelling: An integrated approach. *Language Arts, 69(6)*, 404–408.

Beal, C. R. (1993). Contributions of developmental psychology to understanding revision: Implications for consultation with classroom teachers. *School Psychology Review, 22(4)*, 643–655.

Betts, G. (2004). Fostering autonomous learners through levels of differentiation. *Roeper Review, 26*, 190.

Boss, S. (2002). On the same page: Writing assessment vanguards maintain consistency from coast to coast. *Northwest Education, 8(2)*. Retrieved December 2, 2005, from http://www.nwrel.org/nwedu/08-02/sixtraits/samepage.asp

Bottini, M., & Grossman, S. (2005). Center-based teaching and children's learning: The effects of learning centers on young children's growth and development. *Childhood Education, 81(5)*, 274.

Boyle, O. F., & Peregoy, S. F. (1990). Literacy scaffolds: Strategies for first- and second-language readers. *Reading Teacher, 44(3)*, 194–200.

Butyniec-Thomas, J., & Woloshyn, V. E. (1997). The effects of explicit-strategy and whole-language instruction on students' spelling ability. *Journal of Experimental Education, 65(4)*, 293–302.

Caldwell, J. S., & Ford, M. P. (2002). *Where have all the bluebirds gone? How to soar with flexible grouping.* Portsmouth, NH: Heinemann.

Calkins, L. M. (1986). *The art of teaching writing.* Portsmouth, NH: Heinemann.

Cohen, E. G., Intili, J. K., & Robbins, S. B. (1979). Task and authority: A sociological view of classroom management. In D. Duke (Ed.), *Classroom management: The 78th yearbook of the National Society for the Study of Education* (pp. 116–143). Chicago: University of Chicago Press.

Culham, R. (2004). *Using picture books to teach writing with the traits.* New York: Scholastic Teaching Resources.

Dahl, K., & Farnan, N. (1998). *Children's writing: Perspectives from research.* Newark, DE: International Reading Association.

Dyson, A. H., & Freedman, S. W. (1990). *On teaching writing: A review of the literature* (Occasional Paper No. 20). Berkeley, CA: National Center for the Study of Writing.

Flowers, C. P., Hancock, D. R., & Joyner, R. E. (2000). Effects of instructional strategies and conceptual levels on students' motivation and achievement in a technology course. *Journal of Research and Development in Education, 33(3),* 187–194.

Freedman, S. W., Dyson, A. H., Flower, L., & Chafe, W. (1987). *Research in writing: Past, present and future* (Tech. Rep. No. 1). Berkeley, CA: National Center for the Study of Writing.

Graves, D. H. (1989). *Investigate nonfiction.* Portsmouth, NH: Heinemann.

Harrington, S. L. (1994). An author's storyboard technique as a prewriting strategy. *Reading Teacher, 48(3),* 283–285.

Hillocks, G, (1984). What works in teaching composition: A meta-analysis of experimental treatment studies. *American Journal of Education, 93(1),* 133–170.

Hodapp, A. F., & Hodapp, J. B. (1992) Homework: Making it work. *Intervention in School and Clinic, 27(4),* 233–235.

Hong, E., Milgram, R. M., & Rowell, L. L. (2004). Homework motivation and preference: A learner-centered homework approach. *Theory Into Practice, 43(3),* 197–204.

Hoover, G. (2001). The six traits writing model. *Teachers.net Gazette, 2(2).* Retrieved December 2, 2005, from http://teachers.net/gazette/FEB01/hoover.html

Hudson, S. A. (1988). Children's perceptions of classroom writing: Ownership within a continuum of control. In B. Rafoth & D. Rubin (Eds.), *The social construction of written language* (pp. 37–69). Norwood, NJ: Ablex.

Hughes, J. A. (1991). It really works: Encouraging revision using peer writing tutors. *English Journal, 80(5),* 41–42.

Isernhagen, J., & Kozisek, J. (2000). Improving students' self-perceptions as writers. *Journal of School Improvement, 1(2)*, 3–4.

Kameenui, E. J. (1995). Direct instruction reading as contronym and eononime. *Reading and Writing Quarterly: Overcoming Learning Difficulties, 11(1)*, 3–17.

LeFrancois, G. (2000). *Psychology for teaching* (10th ed.). Belmont, CA: Wadsworth Publishing.

Matsuhashi, A. (1981). Pausing and planning: The tempo of written discourse production. *Research in the Teaching of English, 15(2)*, 113–134.

McCarthey, S. J. (1994). Opportunities and risks of writing from personal experience. *Language Arts, 71(3)*, 182–191.

Morocco, C., & Nelson, A. (1990). *Writers at work: A process approach to writing for grades 4 through 6.* Chicago: Science Research Associates.

Morrow, L. M. (1997). *Literacy development in the early years: Helping children read and write* (3rd ed.). Des Moines, IA: Allyn & Bacon.

Muschla, G. R. (2002). *Writing workshop survival kit.* San Francisco: Jossey-Bass.

Neubert, G. A., & McNelis, S. J. (1990). Peer response: Teaching specific revision suggestions. *English Journal, 79(5)*, 52–56.

Pikiewicz, K., & Sundem, G. (2004). *Implementing an effective writing program.* Huntington Beach, CA: Shell Education.

Radencich, M. C., & McKay, L. J. (1995). *Flexible grouping for literacy in the elementary grades.* Des Moines, IA: Allyn & Bacon.

Ray, K. W. (2001). *The writing workshop: Working through the hard parts (and they're all hard parts).* Urbana, IL: National Council of Teacher of English.

Reed, C. M. (1995). Building editors in the secondary classroom. *Perspectives in Education and Deafness, 13(5)*, 8–10.

Rickards, D., & Cheek, E. (1999). *Designing rubrics for K–6 classroom assessment.* Norwood, MA: Christopher-Gordon.

Rogers, V. (2005). *Some efficient and effective classroom designs that accommodate technology for promoting learning.* Athens: University of Georgia, School Design and Planning Laboratory. (ERIC Document Reproduction Service No. ED485299)

Shalaway, L. (1999). *Learning to teach . . . not just for beginners* (3rd ed.). New York: Scholastic Professional Books.

Spandel, V. (2004). *Creating writers through 6-trait writing assessment and instruction* (4th ed.). Des Moines, IA: Allyn & Bacon.

Steineger, M. (1996). A way with words. *Northwest Education, 2(1),* 20–24.

Tomlinson, C. A. (2004). *How to differentiate instruction in mixed ability classrooms* (2nd ed.). Upper Saddle River, NJ: Prentice Hall.

Weber, C. (2002). *Publishing with students: A comprehensive guide.* Westport, MA: Heinemann.

Wortham, S. C., Barbour, A., & Desjean-Perrotta, B. (1998). *Portfolio assessment.* Olney, MD: Association for Childhood Education International.